A MANUAL OF AKKADIAN

David Marcus
Columbia University

University Press of America™

University Press of America, Inc.™
4710 Auth Place, S.E., Washington, D.C. 20023

Printed in the United States of America

ISBN: 0-8191-0608-9

Library of Congress Catalog Card Number: 78-63068

PREFACE

This Manual is designed to teach Akkadian, the language of ancient Mesopotamia (modern Iraq) to beginning students by the inductive method. By this method the student is immediately introduced to cuneiform writing, and Akkadian grammar is learnt directly as it is encountered. This marks a departure from the usual methods of teaching Akkadian which are either deductive or do not use cuneiform. Moreover this Manual is geared solely for beginners and no background in any other Semitic language is assumed, though occasionally, for purposes of clarification, an example from another Semitic language may be given. The Manual has been used and tested for the past few years in classes at Columbia University, and the author is grateful to all former students who have offered corrections and suggested refinements. The author would also like to acknowledge his debt to Dr. Kenneth L. Barker, his first teacher of Akkadian, to Dr. Moshe Held, his principal mentor and advisor, and to Dr. Edward Greenstein for his constant encouragement and helpful contributions. Gratitude is also expressed to the Biblical Institute Press, Piazza della Pilotta, 35, 00187, Rome, for their kind permission in authorizing use of xerocopies of the excellent cuneiform in T. Bauer, Akkadische Lesestücke published by the Press in 1953.

PREFACE

TABLE OF CONTENTS

INTRODUCTION

0.1 Position of Akkadian

Akkadian belongs to the Semitic family of languages whose chief characteristic is that nearly all verbs can be traced to an original triliteral root (see #1.8).

0.2 Akkadian is East Semitic

According to the traditional geographic division of the Semitic languages Akkadian is classified as East Semitic whereas languages such as Ugaritic, Hebrew, and Phoenician are classified as West Semitic. One of the major distinctions between the two groups is in the verbal system in that Akkadian has two prefix tenses (*iprus* and *iparras*, see #1.11) whereas the West Semitic languages have only one (e.g., Hebrew *yišmōr*, Ugaritic *yqtl*, etc.).

0.3 Dialects of Akkadian

Over the course of its extraordinarily long history (over two and a half thousand years) many recognizable dialects can be distinguished in Akkadian. Some of the chief dialects are: (1) Old Akkadian (OAkk), 2400-2000 B.C.; (2) Old Babylonian (OB), 1950-1595 B.C.; (3) Old Assyrian (OA), 1950-1750 B.C.; (4) Middle Babylonian (MB), 1595-1000 B.C.; (5) Middle Assyrian (MA), 1500-1000 B.C.; (6) Neo-Babylonian (NB), 1000-625 B.C.; (7) Neo-Assyrian (NA), 1000-600 B.C.

0.4 Other dialects

In addition, different dialects can be isolated in texts coming from peripheral areas of Mesopotamia (e.g., the dialects of the

Mari and Amarna letters), and in specific groups of texts (e.g., royal inscriptions). The most common dialect used for literary purposes is that known as Standard Babylonian (SB).

0.5 Dialects used in this Manual

The first dialect dealt with in this Manual is Old Babylonian (OB) which is the language of the Code of Hammurapi, the first text used (chapters 3-11). The second dialect is Standard Babylonian (SB) which is the language of the Descent of Ishtar, the second text (chapters 12-16), and the Annals of Sennacherib, the third text (chapters 17-21).

0.6 Script used in this Manual

The cuneiform script upon which this Manual is based is Neo-Assyrian (NA). The use of the NA script has become a scholarly convention dating back to the time of the early excavations in Mesopotamia when the first script uncovered was that of the Neo-Assyrian period (e.g., the Annals of the Assyrian kings Ashurnasirpal, Sennacherib, Sargon, etc.). It is important to note that while the language in chapters 3-11 is Old Babylonian (based on the text of the Code of Hammurapi), the script is Neo-Assyrian! The rationale for using NA script for the Code of Hammurapi is that it obviates use of a second sign list for beginners.

0.7 How to use the Manual

Since this Manual is based on the inductive method the student is introduced to both cuneiform writing and Akkadian grammar at the same time. Thus the student should try to learn the basic sign list (#1.5) immediately and do the various root exercises given in the early chapters. He, or she, should also attempt to transliterate, normalize, and analyze the text covered by a particular chapter before reading that chapter. After the first two introductory chapters each subsequent chapter is a separate unit containing the grammar of a particular section of text. In the initial chapters every aid is given the student as far as sign list and lexicon are concerned; however, commencing with chapter 8 the student is expected to consult independently the full sign list and glossary. Each chapter contains examples illustrating various parts of grammar. Most of these are taken from the text covered by the particular chapter and can be easily found after working out the text. Other examples, not from the chapter, are accompanied by pertinent textual citations.

Chapter 1

SYLLABLES, BASIC SIGNS, VERBAL SYSTEM

1.1 Cuneiform writing

Akkadian is written in cuneiform which is a logo-syllabic script, that is, made up of a combination of logograms and syllables. Logograms will be discussed in chapter 5 when they are first encountered in the texts (#5.2).

1.2 Syllables

Syllables can be of three types: (1) consisting of a vowel, a, e, i, & u; (2) consisting of a consonant plus a vowel or a vowel plus a consonant, e.g., da, ab, nu, un; (3) consisting of a consonant vowel consonant, e.g., dan, pal, bir.

1.3 Consonants

The following consonants occur in Akkadian: b, d, g, ḫ, k, l, m, n, p, q, r, s, ṣ, š, t, ṭ, w, y, z. Four consonants are not found in English: ḫ, ṭ, ṣ, š. They are pronounced as follows: ḫ, like the ch in 'loch'; ṭ, indistinguishable from t; ṣ, properly a hissing s but normally pronounced ts to distinguish it from s; š, sh as in 'ship'.

1.4 Vowels

There are four vowels in Akkadian: a, e, i, & u, which can be short or long. In our Roman transcription short vowels have no special identifying mark (a, e, i, u), but long vowels are identified by either a macron (ā, ē, ī, ū) or by a circumflex (â, ê, î, û). Vowel length is determined by knowledge of the grammar and the lexicon.

1.5 The basic sign list

The basic sign list contains signs for syllables consisting of
a simple vowel (type 1), or consonant plus vowel or vowel plus
consonant (type 2). The list is arranged alphabetically in
four columns corresponding to the vowels a, e, i, & u.

a	e	i	u
a 𒀀	e 𒂊	i 𒄿	u 𒌋
			ú 𒅇
			ù 𒌓
a','a	e','e	i','i	u','u
ba	be	bi	bu
ab	eb	ib	ub
da	de	di	du
ad	ed	id	ud
ga	ge	gi	gu
ag	eg	ig	ug
ḫa	ḫe	ḫi	ḫu
aḫ	eḫ	iḫ	uḫ
			úḫ
ka	ke	ki	ku
ak	ek	ik	uk
la	le	li	lu
		lí	
al	el	il	ul
ma	me	mi	mu
am	em	im	um
na	ne	ni	nu
an	en	in	un
pa	pe	pi	pu
		pí	
ap	ep	ip	up

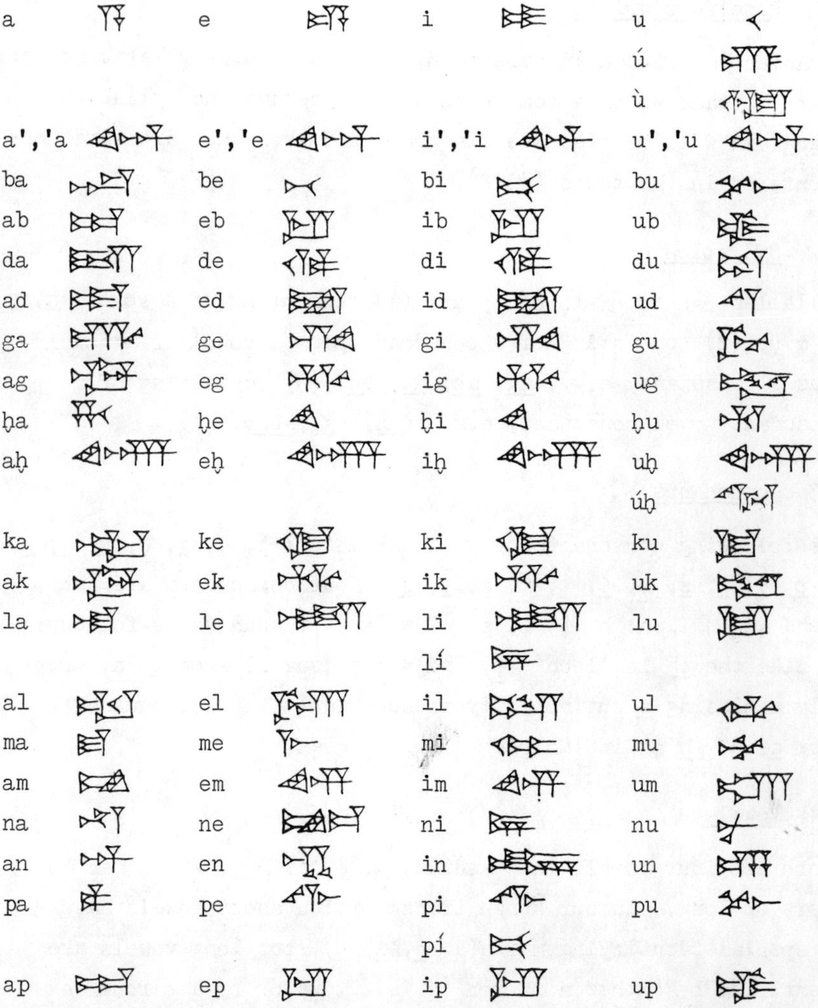

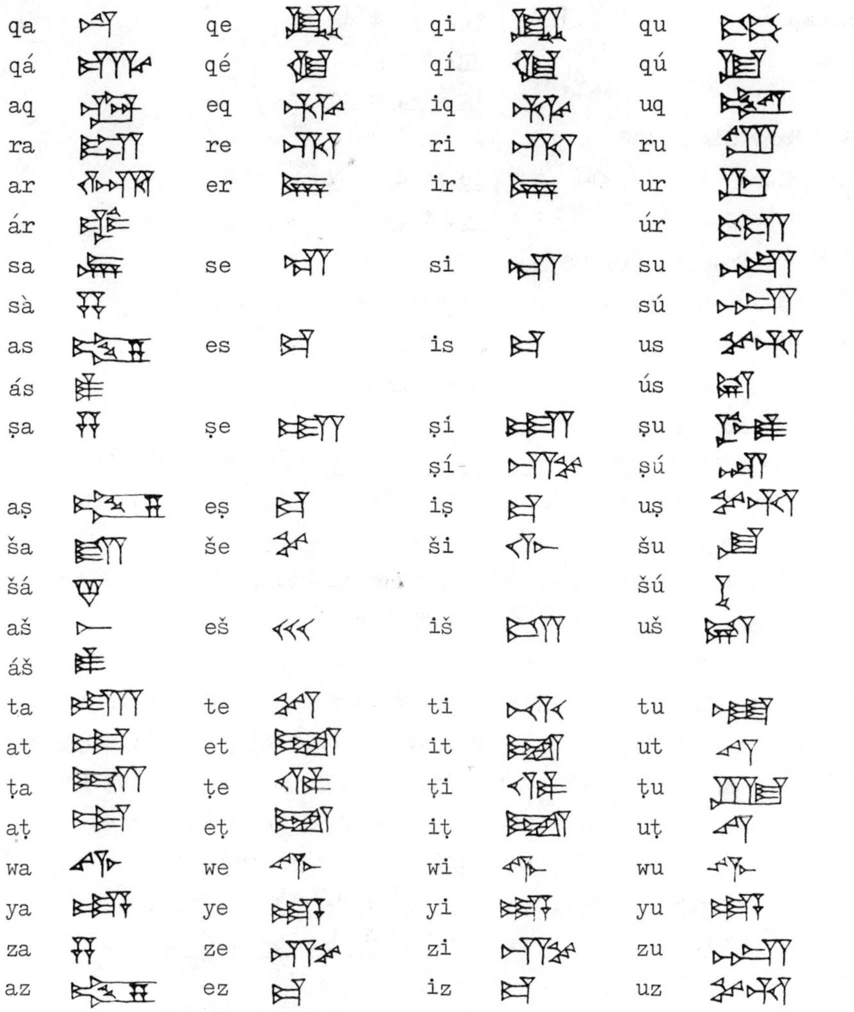
qa qe qi qu
qá qé qí qú
aq eq iq uq
ra re ri ru
ar er ir ur
ár úr
sa se si su
sà sú
as es is us
ás ús
ṣa ṣe ṣi ṣu
ṣí ṣú
aṣ eṣ iṣ uṣ
ša še ši šu
šá šú
aš eš iš uš
áš
ta te ti tu
at et it ut
ṭa ṭe ṭi ṭu
aṭ eṭ iṭ uṭ
wa we wi wu
ya ye yi yu
za ze zi zu
az ez iz uz

1.6 Aids for learning the basic signs

A. In the Neo-Assyrian script there is no distinction at the end of a syllable between voiced, voiceless, and emphatic consonants.

	voiced	voiceless	emphatic
sibilants	z	s	ṣ
dentals	d	t	ṭ
velars	g	k	q
labials	b	p	

Examples:  = *az*, *as*, & *aṣ*

 = *up*, & *ub*

 = *ig*, *ik*, & *iq*

B. Many signs end in *e* or *i*.

Examples:  = *de*, & *di*

 = *ke*, & *ki*

But not *be*, *me*, *še*, or *te*.

C. Many signs begin in either *e* or *i*.

Examples:  = *es*, & *is*

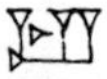 = *eb*, & *ib*

But not *el*, *en*, or *eš*.

D. The sign 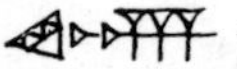 = *aḫ*, *eḫ*, *iḫ*, & *uḫ*. The sign  is used for the glottals *'a*, *a'*, *'e*, *e'*, *'i*, *i'*, *'u*, & *u'*. The sign for *pe*, & *pi*  is used for *wa*, *we*, *wi*, & *wu*.

E. It is suggested that the signs be placed on 3" x 5" cards, each sign on a different card with the sign on the face of the card and the transliteration on the back.

F. Next arrange the signs on other cards according to their physical characteristics, e.g., signs containing the triangular element  or two vertical wedges  should be put together as a series. Make up mnemonics for each different series. For example, for the series containing the character  the signs can be arranged as follows:  *šu*,  *ku*, 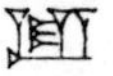 *lu*, 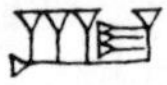 *ṭu*, obtaining the mnemonic *šu-ku-lu-ṭu* = *šukulṭu* "chocolate" !

1.7 Homophonous signs

Many signs in Akkadian represent the same sound. To distinguish them the signs are numbered according to their frequency. A sign which most frequently has a certain value is given that value without any special indication, e.g.,  = *u*; 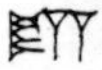 = *ša*. Another sign found less frequently with this value is marked by an acute mark (´) when that sign has this particular value, e.g.,  = *ú*;  = *šá*. A third sign having this value will be indicated with a grave mark (`), e.g., 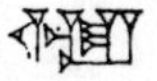 = *ù*; a fourth sign with this value will be denoted by the Arabic numeral 4, e.g.,  = *u*$_4$ (see sign list number 159).

1.8 Triliteral root

One of the major characteristics of Akkadian (and of the Semitic languages in general) is the fact that nearly all verbs can be traced to an original triliteral root. That is, every verb has three root letters which, in the case of strong verbs, will appear in all parts of the verb. Indentification of these root letters is essential in analyzing an Akkadian verbal form.

1.9 Strong verbs

Strong verbs are those whose root letters have three strong consonants. All consonants other than *w* and *y* are considered strong. Some strong verbs are *parāsu* (*prs*), *kašādu* (*kšd*), *šarāku* (*šrk*), etc.

1.10 The paradigm verb

Throughout this Manual the verb *parāsu* 'to cut', which has three strong root letters (*prs*), will be used as the paradigm verb. Note that verbs in Akkadian are listed by their infinitives, so *parāsu* is the infinitive form of the verb whose root letters are *p-r-s*.

1.11 The verbal system

The Akkadian verbal system has three tenses (preterite, present, and stative), four conjugations (designated by the Roman numerals I, II, III, IV), and two infixes (designated by the Arabic numerals 2, 3). The meaning of these will be explained in chapter 7. For the present it will suffice to be familiar with the following 3rd person singular forms which occur in the early laws of Hammurapi.

		TENSE	
		Preterite (= past)	Present (= present or future)
Conjugation	I/1	iprus	iparras
	II/1	uparris	uparras
	III/1	ušapris	ušapras
	IV/1	ipparis	ipparras
Conjugation plus infix	I/2	iptaras	
	II/2	uptarris	

The Arabic numeral 1 alongside the Roman numerals of the conjugation indicates that the form does not have an infix, whereas the Arabic numerals 2 and 3 indicate that the form does have an infix.

1.12 Thematic vowels

The thematic vowels are the vowels between the second and third root letters. In the II/1, III/1, and IV/1 conjugations these vowels are fixed and seldom vary (e.g., the thematic vowel of the preterite is i, that of the present a). However, in the I/1 conjugation the thematic vowels of a given verb vary in both the preterite and present tenses, and will thus always be given in parentheses after the infinitive of the verb. Of the two vowels given the first one indicates the thematic vowel of the present, the second that of the preterite. For example, parāsu has thematic vowels (a, u), so its present is iparras and its preterite iprus. The thematic vowels of šarāqu are (i, i), so it forms its present išarriq and its preterite išriq.

1.13 Roots and conjugational forms

It is imperative for the student to be able to identify roots and conjugations of verbal forms. This is done by comparing the forms under consideration with the paradigm forms of parāsu. Correct conjugational forms of strong verbs may be obtained by simply substituting the three root letters of the verb for the appropriate parāsu form. For example, if one wants to obtain the I/1 present of kašādu one first finds the I/1 present of parāsu (iparras). Then one substitutes the three root letters kšd for the paradigm root letters prs and the form obtained is ikaššad.

1.14 Triliteral root exercise

What are the roots, conjugations, and tenses of the following? For example, ukaššid: root kšd; conjugation II/1; tense preterite.

(1) išakkan (2) uzakkir (3) ušamḫir (4) ušarrak (5) iššakin (6) iššariq (7) išriq (8) ušazkar (9) ušakkan (10) ikaššad (11) ištaraq (12) ikšud (13) iššakkan (14) ušašrak (15) uzannin (16) izzakkar (17) imḫur (18) uktaššid (19) izzannan (20) iznun (21) uštarrik (22) ušarriq (23) umaḫḫir (24) ušaznan (25) ukaššad (26) ušakšid (27) ušašṭar (28) umtaḫḫir (29) iššaṭṭar (30) ušaškin (31) išarrak (32) iktašad (33) imtaḫar (34) umaḫḫar (35) ikkašid (36) ušaṭṭar (37) ušašriq (38) išaṭṭar (39) ištarak (40) uštakkin

Note that some of the above roots in this and future exercises will not be found in the glossary since not all of them occur in the Manual's corpus of texts.

Chapter 2

WEAK VERBS, PHONOLOGICAL RULES, TRANSLITERATION, NORMALIZATION

2.1 Weak verbs

Weak verbs are those verbs in which one or two root letters have dropped out or are liable to drop out. The dropping out of these letters is reflected by the presence of a lengthened or contracted vowel or by the doubling of a letter. There are seven types of weak verbs: (1) initial n, e.g., nadānu; (2) initial w, e.g., wabālu; (3) initial a, e.g., amāru; (4) initial e, e.g., epēšu; (5) middle weak, e.g., dânu; (6) final weak, e.g., banû; (7) double weak, e.g., nadû. When referring to the root form (i.e., the p-r-s form) of a weak verb other than initial n and initial w the weak letter is represented by a glottal stop ' (called aleph) which is then substituted in place of the missing letter. Note that this aleph does not necessarily indicate an etymological Semitic aleph consonant, but only a weak letter which may or may not be equal to an original Semitic aleph consonant.

2.2 Obtaining verbal forms of the weak verbs

The correct conjugational forms of any weak verb may be obtained: (1) by getting the appropriate form of the regular strong verb (parāsu) and substituting the three root letters of the weak verb in place of the p-r-s (same procedure as for strong verbs, see #1.13); (2) by applying the following important rules.

2.3 Rule one

An n at the end of a syllable generally assimilates to the following consonant.

Examples: indin > iddin indi > iddi

However, see #3.12 for some exceptions.

2.4 Rule two

In the I/1 present (iparras) and II/1 preterite (uparris) and present (uparras) of initial weak verbs (initial w, initial a, initial e) the first a drops out.

Examples: I/1 present of wašābu (wšb) (a, i)
Paradigm form is iparras
With substitution of root letters = iwaššab > iwššab
II/1 preterite of ebēru ('br)
Paradigm form is uparris
With substitution of root letters = u'abbir > u'bbir
II/1 present of aḫāzu ('ḫz)
Paradigm form is uparras
With substitution of root letters = u'aḫḫaz > u'ḫḫaz

2.5 Rule three

When an ' (aleph), w, or y closes a syllable the following developments occur:

a' > ā	i' > ī	u' > ū
aw > ū	iw > ū	uw > ū
ay > ī	iy > ī	uy > ū

Examples: idda''ak > iddā'ak iwbil > ūbil
irayyab > irīyab i'ḫuz > īḫuz

A similar change occurs when an ' (aleph) opens a syllable, e.g., 'a > ā; 'i > ī; 'u > ū.

Examples: iš'am > išām id'in > idīn id'uk > idūk

2.6 Rule four

Two vowels separated by an **'** (aleph), **w**, or **y** contract into the second vowel. A circumflex indicates the contraction.

Examples: iddā'ak > iddâk   uktā'in > uktîn
           irīyab > irâb

2.7 Rule five

Long vowels preceding double consonants are shortened.

Examples: ūbbir > ubbir   īḫḫaz > iḫḫaz

2.8 Rule six

A short vowel in the middle of two consonants which are flanked by short vowels will drop out.

Examples: ḫaliqu > ḫalqu   ṣabitu > ṣabtu

2.9 Rule seven

At the end of final weak forms long vowels indicated by a macron (but never contracted vowels indicated by a circumflex) are shortened.

Examples: ibnī > ibni   iddī > iddi

With the addition of another syllable the long vowel is retained, e.g., ibnīšu, iddīma.

2.10 Examples of weak verbs and the rules

With the following verbs the appropriate form of parāsu is first obtained. Thus to form the I/1 preterite of nadānu (i, i) the appropriate preterite form is ipris (remember that the thematic vowels vary in the I/1, the conjugation of all the examples below). The three root letters of the weak verb are then substituted in place of p-r-s, e.g., in our example, n-d-n for p-r-s, ipris, indin. Next the rules are followed and the numbers after the verbal forms refer to the rules which were applied. In our example only rule one applies, so indin becomes iddin.

Initial n *nadānu* (*i*, *i*) *ipris* *indin* > *iddin* (1)
iparris *inaddin*

Initial w *wašābu* (*a*, *i*) *ipris* *iwšib* > *ūšib* (3)
iparras *iwaššab* > *iwššab* (2) >
ūššab (3) > *uššab* (5)

Initial a *aḫāzu* (*a*, *u*) *iprus* *i'ḫuz* > *īḫuz* (3)
iparras *i'aḫḫaz* > *i'ḫḫaz* (2) >
īḫḫaz (3) > *iḫḫaz* (5)

Initial e *epēšu* (*e*, *u*) *iprus* *i'puš* > *īpuš* (3)
iparreš *i'appeš* > *i'ppeš* (2) >
īppeš (3) > *ippeš* (5)

Middle weak *dânu* (*a*, *i*) *ipris* *id'in* > *idīn* (3)
iparras *ida''an* > *idā'an* (3) >
idân (4)

Final weak *banû* (*i*, *i*) *ipris* *ibni'* > *ibnī* (3) > *ibni* (7)
iparris *ibanni'* > *ibannī* (3) >
ibanni (7)

Double weak *nadû* (*i*, *i*) *ipris* *indi'* > *iddi'* (1) > *iddī* (3)
> *iddi* (7)
iparris *inaddi'* > *inaddī* (3) >
inaddi (7)

2.11 Rules applied in sequence

It will be noted that the rules where applicable are followed in sequence. For example, rule two is applied before rules three or four. Thus, in a form like *u'abbir* rule two is applied first (which results in *u'bbir*, then *ūbbir* [rule three], then *ubbir* [rule five]), not rule four (which would result in *âbbir*, then *abbir* [rule five]).

2.12 Transliteration

The first stage in presenting an Akkadian text is transliteration, putting the cuneiform signs into their correct Latin equivalents, e.g.,  = *bi*. In many syllables there is no distinction between voiced, voiceless, and emphatic consonants (#1.6), e.g.,  = *az*, *as*, & *aṣ*;  = *ig*, *ik*, & *iq*, but only one of these values can be selected for the transliteration. Likewise only one value can be chosen between syllables beginning or ending in *e* or *i* (#1.6b,c), e.g., *eb* or *ib*, *de* or *di*.

2.13 Normalization

Normalization is the putting together of the transliterated syllables to make Akkadian words, e.g., *a-wi-lum* = *awîlum*. In this stage the transliterated consonants are always indicated but the vowels coalesce. For example, the word *da-an-num* is normalized *dannum*, the two *n* consonants are written but only one *a* vowel. Consonantal and vowel harmony can be clearly seen at this stage. However, where two different vowels come together in a word they both must be indicated in the normalization, e.g., *ú-ṣí-a-am-ma* > *ūṣi'amma* (CH 3).

2.14 Agreement in normalization

Generally in a word there is agreement in normalization between the final vowel or consonant of one sign and the initial vowel or consonant of the following sign. For example, in the word *ib-ba-aš-šu-ú* (CH 5) the sign  has the values *ib* and *ip*, but the sign which follows 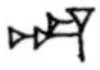 can only be read *ba*, (and not *pa*, which is ). Thus consonantal harmony shows the reading *ib-ba* to be the correct one. In the word *ne-er-tam* (CH 1) the sign  can be read *er* or *ir*, but the sign which precedes  can only be read *ne* (and not *ni*, which is ), so the correct selection is *er*. Where the principle of harmony leads to more than one possibility then only knowledge of grammar and the lexicon determines the correct reading. For example, in the word *id-da-ak* (CH 1), the sign  can be read *ed*, *id*, *et*, *it*, *eṭ*, or *iṭ*, but since the following sign  has only the readings *da* and *ṭa* only one set (*et* and *it*) can be eliminated. The reading *id-da-ak* is chosen on grammatical and lexical grounds: on grammatical grounds because the verbal prefix in Akkadian starts with *i* not *e*, hence *id* not *ed*; on lexical grounds because the word *id-da-ak* (*iddâk*) comes from a root *d'k*, and there is no root *t'k* in Akkadian.

2.15 Vowel length in normalization

The correct grammatical and lexical long accents (macrons or circumflexes) must be inserted in the normalization. For example, *id-da-ak* is normalized *iddâk*, the circumflex indicating the conjugation and root of the verb. The word *a-wi-lum* is normalized *awīlum*, the macron over the *i* indicating a long vowel. Vowel length is determined by knowledge of the grammar and the lexicon. A clue to the usage of the macron and the circumflex is that the latter is only used for contracted vowels (#2.6).

2.16 Extra vowel-signs and vowel length

Extra vowel-signs may or may not indicate vowel length. For example, the word *ú-ul* is normalized *ul*, there being no vowel length in spite of the extra vowel-sign. The word *di-nu-um* is normalized *dīnum*, the two *u* vowels do not indicate length, but the *i* is long for lexical reasons. However, in both *šu-ú* (*šû*) and *iq-bu-ú* (*iqbû*) the extra vowels indicate length.

2.17 Indication of homophones

The number of the frequency of homophonic values (#1.7) is indicated in the transliteration but not in the normalization. For example, the number of the homophone *u* is indicated in the transliteration of the word *ú-ub-bi-ir-ma* but not in the normalization *ubbirma* (not *úbbirma*). Similarly the number of the homophone *sà* is written in the transliteration but not in the normalization of *sarrātim* (not *sàrrātim*).

2.18 Polyphonous signs

When a sign represents a number of different values that sign is said to be polyphonous. For example, the sign 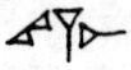 has the values *pe*, *pi*, *wa*, *we*, *wi*, & *wu*; the sign  has, among others, the values *ut* and *tam*. When dealing with a polyphonous sign the correct value must be selected for the transliteration. This is determined by elimination based on vowel and consonantal harmony, and on a knowledge of the grammar and the lexicon.

Chapter 3

THE CODE OF HAMMURAPI
Law One

3.0 Law one

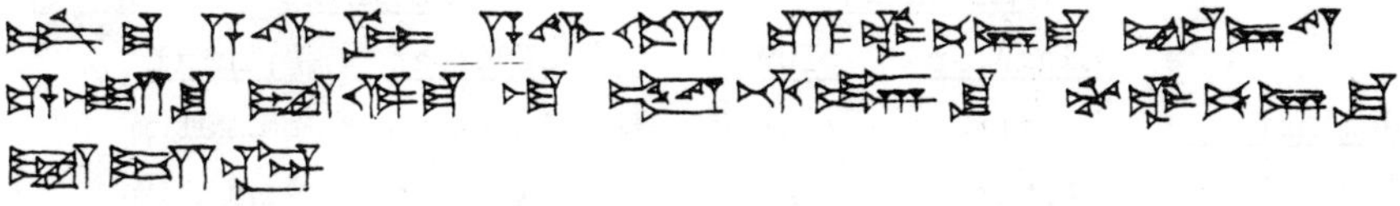

Transliterate (#2.12) and normalize (#2.13) the above using the basic sign list (#1.5) and the following additional signs:

 *šum* (63)  *lum* (221)  *lam* (182)

 *tam* (159 = *ud/ut/uṭ*)

The numbers refer to the sign list at the back of the Manual.

3.1 Vocabulary of law one

Nouns: *awīlum* 'a man', *nertum* 'murder charge', *mubbirum* 'an accuser'.

Verbs: *'br* (*ebēru*) II/1 'to accuse'

nd' (*nadû*) I/1 (*i*, *i*) 'to bring' (lit. 'to hurl')

k'n (*kânu*) II/2 'to convict'

d'k (*dâku*) IV/1 'to be executed'

Adverb: *lā* 'not'

Conjunctions: *šumma* 'if', *ma* 'and', 'but'.

Preposition: *eli* 'against'

3.2 The conjunction šumma

The conjunction šumma 'if', which occurs in the protasis of many of the laws, is normally followed by a verb in the preterite tense. For example, šumma awīlum awīlam ubbir "If a man accused (another) man."

3.3 The noun

The noun has two genders (masculine and feminine), three numbers (singular, plural, and dual), and three cases (nominative, accusative, and genitive).

3.4 Paradigm of the noun

	Masculine		Feminine	
	singular	plural	singluar	plural
Nominative	šarrum	šarrū	šarratum	šarrātum
Accusative	šarram	šarrī	šarratam	šarrātim
Genitive	šarrim	šarrī	šarratim	šarrātim

3.5 Gender of the noun

The noun šarrum 'king' is masculine; šarratum 'queen' feminine. Feminine nouns are identified: (a) by being naturally feminine, e.g., ummum 'mother'; (b) by a t or at ending, e.g., nertum 'murder charge', awatum 'word'.

3.6 Number of the noun

There are three numbers of the noun: singular, plural, and dual (which will be discussed later). In Old Babylonian (OB) the singular noun is characterized by mimation---an m occurring after the case vowel. The chief characteristics of the plural are: (a) the lengthening of the ultimate vowel in masculine nouns; (b) the lengthening of the penultimate vowel in feminine nouns. Note that the masculine plural noun does not have mimation (šarrū), but the feminine plural noun does (šarrātum).

3.7 Use of mimation in the Manual

Since mimation does not normally occur in Standard Babylonian (SB) (however, see #13.2), it will be indicated only on nouns which occur in the Old Babylonian section of the Manual, that is, through chapter 11. In the glossary, to avoid confusion between the two dialects, mimation has not been indicated at all but should be assumed for all nouns that are found in OB.

3.8 Cases of the noun

There are three cases of the noun: nominative, accusative, and genitive. The nominative is used when the noun is the subject of a sentence; the accusative is used when the noun is the object of a sentence. For example, šumma awīlum awīlam ubbir "If a man accused (another) man." The genitive is used when the noun is preceded by a preposition (#4.2) or by a construct (#4.4). The term "oblique" is used by grammarians to refer to both the accusative and genitive cases, especially in the plural. Thus šarrī and šarrātim are oblique cases.

3.9 Enclitic ma

The conjunction ma 'and', 'but' is normally attached to the last word preceding the clause it introduces. For example, šumma awīlum awīlam ubbirma nertam elīšu iddīma lā uktînšu "If a man accused (another) man and has brought against him a charge of murder, but has not convicted him." Note that if ma is added to a word ending in a vowel that vowel is lengthened, e.g., ukannūšu + ma = ukannūšūma (CH 5).

3.10 Pronominal suffixes

Pronominal suffixes may be attached to nouns, verbs, and prepositions. One of the most frequent encountered in the early laws is šu 'his', 'him', e.g., elīšu 'against him', uktînšu 'convicted him', mubbiršu 'his accuser'.

3.11 The negative lā

The negative *lā* 'not' is used in subordinate clauses (including conditional clauses) and to negate imperatives.

3.12 Some exceptions to rule one (#2.3)

There are some exceptions to the rule that an *n* at the end of a syllable assimilates to the following consonant (#2.3). For example, when an *n* is the last consonant of a word it will not normally assimilate before a pronominal suffix or enclitic *ma*. Examples: *ukînšu*, *dīnšu* (CH 5), *innaddinma* (CH 29). However, note *iddiššum* < *iddinšum* (CH 17).

3.13 Sumerian influence on word order

The placement of the verb at the end of the sentence (e.g., *šumma awīlum awīlam ubbirma*; *nērtam elīšu iddīma*; *mubbiršu iddâk*) is a syntactic feature representing an Akkadian borrowing from Sumerian.

3.14 Root exercise

What are the roots, conjugations, and tenses of the following? (1) *īḫuz* (2) *ubbar* (3) *iddin* (4) *ušūbil* (5) *ibni* (6) *ukîn* (7) *uššab* (8) *ūbil* (9) *irâm* (10) *ušāḫiz*.

3.15 Transliteration of law one

šum-ma a-wi-lum a-wi-lam ú-ub-bi-ir-ma ne-er-tam e-li-šu id-di-ma la uk-ti-in-šu mu-ub-bi-ir-šu id-da-ak

3.16 Normalization of law one

šumma awīlum awīlam ubbirma nertam elīšu iddīma lā uktînšu mubbiršu iddâk

3.17 Translation of law one

If a man accused (another) man and has brought against him a charge of murder, but has not convicted him, his accuser shall be executed.

Chapter 4

THE CODE OF HAMMURAPI
Law Three

4.0 Law three

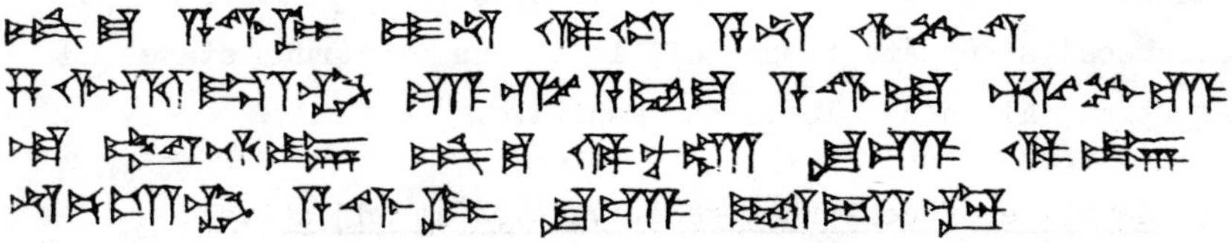

Transliterate and normalize the above using the basic sign list and the following additional signs:

 *šum* (63)  *lum* (221)  *nim* (180)

 *tim* (47)

4.1 Vocabulary of law three

Nouns: *dīnum* 'law case', *šībūtum* 'testimony', *sarrātum* 'falsehood', *awatum* 'word', *napištum* 'life'.

Pronoun: *šû* 'he', 'that'

Verbs: *wṣ'* (*waṣû*) I/1 (*i*, *i*) 'to go out'

qb' (*qabû*) I/1 (*i*, *i*) 'to speak'

Prepositions: *ina* 'in', *ana* 'for the purpose of'.

4.2 Prepositions govern the genitive case

After a preposition the noun appears in the genitive case (#3.8). Examples: *ina dīnim* 'in the case', *eli awīlim* 'against the man', *itti dayyānī* 'with the judges'.

4.3 Abstract ūtum ending

When added to a noun the ending ūtum gives it an abstract meaning. Examples: šarrum 'king', šarrūtum 'kingship'; šībum 'witness', šībūtum 'testimony'.

4.4 Construct-genitive phrase

In the phrase bīt awīlim 'house of the man' the first word bīt 'house of' is in the construct state while the second word awīlim 'the man' is in the genitive (#3.8). In this construct-genitive phrase the two words together make up a compound idea "the man's house". Similarly in šībūt sarrātim 'testimony of falsehood' šībūt 'testimony of' is in the construct state and sarrātim 'falsehood' is in the genitive.

4.5 Genitive of construct-genitive used as adjective

Many times the noun of the genitive in a construct-genitive phrase can simply be translated as an adjective qualifying the construct noun, e.g., šībūt sarrātim 'testimony of falsehood' or 'false testimony'.

4.6 Construct-genitive not subject to normal case endings

A construct-genitive phrase can occur anywhere in a sentence but, because it is a separate phrase, it is not subject to the normal case endings. For example, in the following sentences the phrase mār šarrim 'son of the king' = 'the king's son' occurs in all three cases without any change of form.

Nominative: mār šarrim ana ēkallim illik "the king's son went to the palace"

Accusative: awīlum mār šarrim imḫaṣ "the man struck the king's son"

Genitive: ana mār šarrim kaspam iddin "he gave money to the king's son"

Likewise in ana šībūt sarrātim "for the purpose of false testimony", šībūt does not take the expected genitive case after a preposition (#4.2) because it is in a construct-genitive phrase.

4.7 More than one construct or genitive in a construct-genitive phrase

There can be more than one construct or genitive form in a construct-genitive phrase. For example, qāt mār šarrim "the hand of the king's son"; šībūt še'im u kaspim "testimony concerning grain or money" (CH 4).

4.8 Formation of the construct

The construct is obtained either by dropping case endings or by using the genitive form.

4.9 Dropping case endings (including mimation)

A. With regular nouns:

Nominative		Construct	
bēlum	'lord'	bēl	'lord of'
dīnum	'case'	dīn	'case of'
awīlum	'man'	awīl	'man of'

B. With geminate nouns:

In the case of many geminate nouns (nouns whose ultimate and penultimate consonants are identical) the last consonant is also dropped.

Nominative		Construct	
šarrum	'king'	šar	'king of'
kunukkum	'seal'	kunuk	'seal of'

C. With nouns containing two syllables:

In two syllabic nouns of a type like parsum, pirsum, or pursum and in some feminine nouns anaptyxis (the addition of a vowel between the last two consonants) takes place. Generally there is vowel harmony so that the additional vowel (the anaptyctic vowel) will agree with the vowel in the first syllable.

Nominative		Construct
wardum	'slave'	*ward* > *warad*
niksum	'cutting'	*niks* > *nikis*
uznum	'ear'	*uzn* > *uzun*

In feminine forms the anaptyctic vowel is *a*

šubtum	'dwelling'	*šubt* > *šubat*
šimtum	'fate'	*šimt* > *šimat*

4.10 Using the genitive form (without mimation)

Nominative		Construct	
abum	'father'	*abi*	'father of'
mimmûm	'property'	*mimmî*	'property of'
šarrū	'kings'	*šarrī*	'kings of'

4.11 The ventive am

The ventive *am* is a suffix attached to verbal forms like *iprus*, e.g., *iprusam*. Its effect is to give the verb a dative or special lexical meaning.

4.12 Dative meaning of ventive am

Here the ventive means 'to me'.

išruk	'he gave'	*išrukam*	'he gave to me'
išpur	'he sent'	*išpuram*	'he sent to me'

4.13 Lexical meaning of ventive am

Here the ventive *am* has the effect of connoting action here as opposed to action there.

ūṣi 'he went' (there) = 'he went out'
ūṣi'am 'he went' (here) = 'he came'
illik 'he went' (there) = 'he went away'
illikam 'he went' (here) = 'he came'

4.14 Uncontracted vowels in OB

Frequently in Old Babylonian (OB) vowels will remain uncontracted, that is they do not contract, according to rule four (#2.6), to the second vowel. For example, in the word *ūṣi'amma* the vowels *i* and *a* are uncontracted and do not go, according to rule four, to *a*. In the later language *ūṣi'am* will go to *ūṣâ*. An *aleph* sign is normally inserted between two such uncontracted vowels. Other examples: *ušalli'amma* (CH 2), *uštēṣi'am* (CH 16), *irtedi'aššu* (CH 17).

4.15 The subjunctive

Unlike the Indo-European languages where the subjunctive expresses a thought or wish, the subjunctive in Akkadian is simply a term for a *u* vowel which is added to a verb in a subordinate clause. The most common introducer of subordinate clauses is the relative pronoun *ša* 'who', 'which', 'what'. Examples of the subjunctive: *awātim ša iqbû* "the words which he spoke"; *kaspam ša išqulu ileqqe* "he shall take the money which he paid" (CH 9).

4.16 Dropping of the relative pronoun ša

If the relative pronoun *ša* is dropped then the noun preceding it will appear in the construct case. Examples:

awāt iqbû < *awātim ša iqbû* "the words which he spoke"

ina dīn idīnu < *ina dīnim ša idīnu* "for (changing) the case which he judged" (CH 5)

kasap išqulu < *kaspam ša išqulu* "the money which he paid" (CH 9)

4.17 Independent pronouns used demonstratively

The third person independent pronouns *šû* 'he', *šî* 'she', *šunu* 'they' (masc.), *šina* 'they' (fem.) can be used as demonstratives. Examples: *awīlum šû iddâk* "that man shall be executed"; *sinništum šî* "that woman".

4.18 Root exercise

What are the roots, conjugations, and tenses of the following? (1) idīn (2) itbal (3) ušamqat (4) irdi (5) idân (6) ukân (7) itâr (8) inaddi (9) ištakan (10) išām (11) ubbir (12) ukîn

4.19 Transliteration of law three

šum-ma a-wi-lum i-na di-nim a-na ši-bu-ut sà-ar-ra-tim ú-ṣí-a-am-ma a-wa-at iq-bu-ú la uk-ti-in šum-ma di-nu-um šu-ú di-in na-pí-iš-tim a-wi-lum šu-ú id-da-ak

4.20 Normalization of law three

šumma awīlum ina dīnim ana sibūt sarrātim ūṣi'amma awāt iqbû lā uktîn šumma dīnum šû dīn napištim awīlum šû iddâk

4.21 Translation of law three

If a man has come forward in a law case for the purpose of (giving) false testimony, but has not proven the words which he spoke, if that case is a capital one, that man shall be executed.

Chapter 5

THE CODE OF HAMMURAPI
Law Four

5.0 Law four

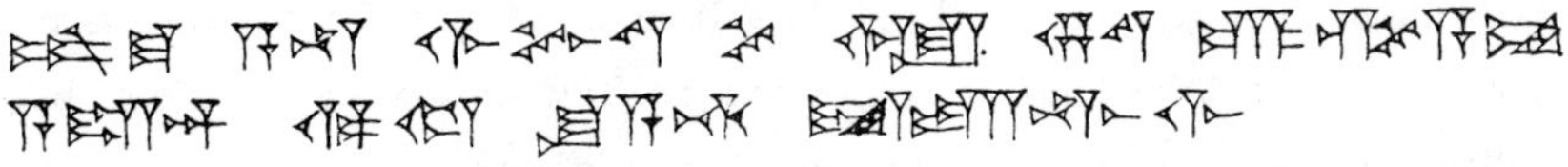

Transliterate and normalize the above using the basic sign list and the following additional signs:
 *šum* (63)  ŠE = *še'um* (150)  KÙ.BABBAR = *kaspum* (196)  *nim* (180)

5.1 Vocabulary of law four

Nouns: *še'um* 'grain', *kaspum* 'silver', 'money', *arnum* 'penalty'.
Pronoun: *šu'āti* 'that'
Verb: *nš'* (*našû*) I/3 (i, i) 'to bear'
Conjunction: *u* 'and', 'or'

5.2 Logograms

A logogram is a Sumerian word represented by one sign in the case of a simple logogram or by two or more signs in the case of a composite logogram.

5.3 Simple logogram

A simple logogram is represented by only one sign. Examples:
 É = *bītum* 'house'  GAL = *rabûm* 'great'
 ŠE = *še'um* 'grain'  KUR = *mātum* 'land'

Note that a logogram is written in capital letters in the transliteration and is replaced by the correct Akkadian equivalent in the normalization.

5.4 Composite logogram

A composite logogram is represented by two or more signs.

 KÙ.BABBAR = *kaspum* 'silver', 'money'

 É.GAL = *ēkallum* 'palace'

5.5 Logograms in the sign list

In the sign list at the back of the Manual simple logograms can be found in the third column, composite logograms in the fourth. The first column indicates the cuneiform sign, the second column the syllabic value or values of that sign. For example, the cuneiform sign 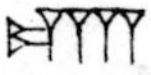 (127) can be read syllabically as *bit* or *é*; as a simple logogram as É = *bītum* 'house'; as a composite logogram with the sign  as É.GAL = *ēkallum* 'palace'. Similarly the cuneiform sign  (225) can be read syllabically as *a*; as a simple logogram as A = *aplum* 'heir' or A = *mû* 'water'; as a composite logogram with the sign  as A.ŠÀ = *eqlum* 'field'.

5.6 Normalizing logograms

The Akkadian equivalents of logograms must be put into the correct case in the normalization. For example, after *šībūt* in law four the Akkadian equivalent of ŠE must appear in the genitive case because *šībūt* is the construct part of a construct-genitive phrase (#4.4).

5.7 Recognizing logograms in the text

Logograms can be recognized in the cuneiform text in two ways: (1) by the fact that the sign has no syllabic value; (2) by the fact that the syllabic reading of the sign makes no sense in context. Thus the sign  (196) has no syllabic value in the corpus of texts included in this Manual so it will not be found in the first column of the sign list. Alternatively, the sign  (150) which does have a syllabic value (*še*) cannot be read *še* in the context of law four (see #5.6). When dealing with a logogram in the sign list one should always check the fourth column to be certain that the sign is not part of a composite logogram. For example, the sign  (231) can be read as a simple logogram NINDA = *akalum* 'food' but if it is followed by the sign 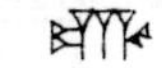 it has to be read NÍG.GA = *makkūrum* 'property'.

5.8 Cases of the independent pronoun

The independent pronoun has three cases: nominative, genitive/accusative, and dative. For example, the 3rd person masculine singular has the following three cases: nominative *šû*, genitive/accusative *šu'āti*, dative *šu'āšim*. The full paradigm of the independent pronoun is given in #13.7.

5.9 Infixes

Akkadian has two verbal infixes: a *t* infix and a *tan* infix. The former is represented by the Arabic numeral 2 (#1.11), the latter is represented by the Arabic numeral 3. The I/2 preterite of *parāsu* is *iptaras*, the I/2 present is *iptarras*. The I/3 preterite is *iptarras* (< *iptanras*), the I/3 present is *iptanarras*. The thematic vowels (#1.12) of these infixes are the same as the I/1 present. For example, the I/1 present of *našû* (*i*, *i*) is *inašši*, the I/3 preterite is *ittašši*, the I/3 present is *ittanašši*.

5.10 Root exercise

What are the roots, conjugations, and tenses of the following?

(1) *idân* (2) *ušamqit* (3) *uktîn* (4) *inaddi* (5) *itūr* (6) *iqbi*

(7) *ištanakkan* (8) *ištaqqal* (9) *illak* (10) *išâm* (11) *iqtabi*

5.11 Transliteration of law four

šum-ma a-na ši-bu-ut ŠE *ù* KÙ.BABBAR *ú-ṣí-a-am a-ra-an di-nim* šu-a-ti it-ta-na-aš-ši

5.12 Normalization of law four

šumma ana šībūt še'im u kaspim ūṣi'am aran dīnim šu'āti ittanašši

5.13 Translation of law four

If he has come forward for the purpose of (false) testimony concerning grain or money, he shall bear the penalty of that case.

Chapter 6

THE CODE OF HAMMURAPI
Law Five

6.0 Law five

Transliterate and normalize the above using the basic sign list and the following additional signs:

 šum (63)  nam (38)  kam (168)  nim (180) 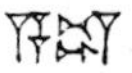 A.RÁ = adi (225)  U.MIN = šinšer (173)  GIŠ = iṣum (112) 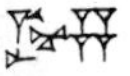 GU.ZA = kussûm (217)

6.1 Vocabulary of law five

Nouns: dayyānum 'judge', dīnum 'verdict', kunukkum 'sealed document', purussûm 'decision', rugummûm 'claim', puḫrum 'assembly', kussûm 'seat', dayyānūtum 'judgeship', šinšer 'twelve'.

Pronoun: ša 'who', 'which', 'what'

Verbs: d'n (dânu) I/1 (a, i) 'to try (a case)'

prs (parāsu) I/1 (a, u) 'to render (a decision)'

'zb (ezēbu) III/1 'to have (a sealed document) made out'

'n' (*enû*) I/1 I/2 (*i*, *i*) 'to change'

bš' (*bašû*) IV/1 'to be'

ndn (*nadānu*) I/1 (*i*, *i*) 'to give', 'to pay'

tb' (*tebû*) III/1 'to remove'

t'r (*târu*) I/1 (*a*, *u*) 'to return'

wšb (*wašābu*) I/1 (*a*, *i*) 'to sit'

Adverbs: *warkânum* 'afterwards', *ul* 'not'.

Prepositions: *adi* 'up to', *itti* 'with'.

6.2 The writing a-a for aya or ayya

The writing *a-a* often represents *aya* or *ayya*. For example, *da-a-a-nu-um* 'judge' is to be normalized *dayyānum* (Cf. Ugaritic *dyn*, Hebrew *dayyān*, etc.). Likewise, *ša-a-a-ma-nu-um* (CH 9) is to be normalized *šayyāmānum* 'that buyer' (< *šayyāmum* 'a buyer').

6.3 Nomen agentis forms

Nomen agentis forms (nouns which denote professions) are found in the I, II, and III conjugations. The regular *nomen agentis* form of the II conjugation is *parrāsum*. Forms of this type which are found in the early laws are *dayyānum* 'judge', *šarrāqum* 'thief', *šayyāmum* 'buyer'.

6.4 Defective writing

Sometimes words are written defectively in the cuneiform. Thus *purussûm* is written with only one *s*. It should be correctly normalized with two *s*'s. Similarly *maṣṣarūtum* in law 7 is written with only one *ṣ*. The correct forms can be obtained from the glossary.

6.5 Cognate accusatives

A common feature of all the Semitic languages is the use of a verb with its cognate accusative. The latter is a noun which is derived from the verb with which it is associated. For example, *dīnum* + *dânu* 'to try a case', *purussûm* + *parāsu* 'to render a decision'.

6.6 The e vowel

An *e* vowel in Akkadian developed from an original *a* or *i* vowel which became *e* due to there being a liquid letter (*l*, *m*, *n*, *r*) in a word or because of there originally having been a laryngeal which has dropped out. Examples of occurrences of an *e* vowel due to a liquid letter are: *lemēnu* < *lamānu*, *šebēru* < *šabāru*, *qebēru* < *qabāru*. Examples of an *e* vowel reflecting a lost laryngeal are: *ezēbu* < *azābu* (original *ʿ* [*ayin*] dropped out), *ušēzib* < *ušaʿzib*, *īteni* < *iʿtani*. An *e* vowel also is found in some Sumerian loan words in Akkadian, e.g., APIN = *epinnum* 'plow'.

6.7 Affect on other vowels

The force of the liquid letters and the original laryngeals affects other vowels in a word as well. For example, in *tebû* (< *tabû*) even though the original laryngeal dropped at the end of the word it is reflected in the first vowel. Likewise in *enêm* (< *ʿanîm*) both vowels have changed to *e*.

6.8 Original laryngeal can be traced

The original laryngeal can frequently be traced by comparison with other Semitic languages, e.g., *ezēbu* corresponds to Hebrew *ʿāzab* so that the original laryngeal was an *ʿ* (*ayin*) and the original root letters were *ʿzb*. Remember though that for purposes of indicating verbal roots and working out forms of weak verbs the laryngeal is represented in the Manual by an *'* (*aleph*) sign (#2.1). Thus the root letters of *ezēbu* will be found in the glossary under *'zb* (not under *ʿzb*). Sometimes the exact laryngeal is unknown to us though the *e* vowel shows one to have been somewhere in the root. On the basis of Late Hebrew *ʿānā* 'to change' the original root letters of the verb *enû* were apparently *ʿny*.

6.9 Adverbial ending ânum

The element ânum when attached to a preposition gives it adverbial force. Thus warki 'after', warkânum 'afterwards'.

6.10 Infixed t in šumma clauses

There is a tendency for the last verb in a šumma clause to be an infixed t form. Examples: šumma awīlum awīlam ubbirma nertam elīšu iddīma lā uktînšu (CH 1); šumma dayyānum dīnam idīn purussâm iprus kunukkam ušēzib warkânumma dīnšu iteni.

6.11 Casus pendens

A casus pendens (the hanging or dangling case of the noun) is best translated by 'as for', 'as regards'. It normally occurs in the oblique case and is always followed by a resumptive pronominal suffix. Examples: dayyānam šu'āti...ukannūšu "as for that judge ...they shall convict him"; šumma awīlam šu'āti dId ūtebbibaššu "if, as for that man, the River-god declared him innocent" (CH 2). It is important to note that the pronominal suffix refers back to the casus pendens. Thus with a feminine subject the suffix would be feminine, e.g., šarratim...ukannūši; with a plural subject the suffix would be plural, e.g., šarrū...ukannūšunūti.

6.12 Declension of infinitive

The infinitive can be declined like a noun, e.g., parāsum, parāsam, parāsim. After a preposition the infinitive will then appear in the genitive case (#4.2), for example, ina...enêm "for changing...".

6.13 Object of the infinitive

There are three ways of representing an object in an infinitive clause: (1) by preceding the verb in the accusative case; (2) by preceding the verb in the genitive case if it is itself preceded by a preposition; (3) by following the verb in a construct-genitive relationship. For example, the phrase "to (ana) plow (erēšu) the field (eqlum)" can be expressed either (1) eqlam ana erēšim; or (2) ana eqlim erēšim; or (3) ana erēš eqlim. The phrase ina dīn idīnu enêm is an infinitive clause of type 2, the object of the infinitive being the relative clause dīn idīnu (which stands for dīnim ša idīnu, #4.16).

6.14 Third person plural

The third person masculine plural forms are: preterite iprusū, present iparrasū. As in other Semitic languages and in English, the third person plural can have an impersonal passive connotation, e.g., 'they say' = 'it is said', ukannūšu "they shall convict him" = "he shall be convicted."

6.15 Middle weak verbs with vocalic affixes

With the addition of vocalic affixes to the present of middle weak verbs the third root letter is doubled. For example, the II/1 third masculine singular present of k'n (kânu) is ukân. In the plural ukânū becomes ukannū. Note that long vowels preceding double consonants are shortened (#2.7).

6.16 The relative pronoun ša

One of the primary usages of the pronoun ša is as a relative 'who', 'which', 'what', for example, rugummâm ša ina dīnim šu'āti ibbaššû "the claim which is in that case." Note that ša as a relative pronoun must be followed by the subjunctive u (#4.15).

6.17 The multiplier šu

The suffix šu is used with the adverbial ending ī to indicate "times", e.g., adi šinšerīšu inaddin "he shall pay up to twelve times."

6.18 Signs for the numbers

The following signs represent the numbers occurring in the

Manual's corpus of texts:

1		(201)	10		(173)
2		(222)	12		(173)
3		(229)	20		(198)
4		(231)	30		(199)
		(62)	50		(200)
5		(232)	60		(201)
6		(233)	100		(206)
7		(234)	1000		(188)
8		(235)			

For the usages of these signs, see #18.7.

6.19 Numbers in the early laws

Numbers met with in the early laws are:

1 = *ištēn* (*ištēn mana kaspam* "one mina of silver" CH 24)
2 = *šinā* (*šinā šiqil kaspam* "two shekels of silver" CH 17)
5 = *ḫamšum* (*adi ḫamšīšu* "up to five times" CH 12)
6 = *šeššum* (*ana/ina šeššet warḫī* "up to/within six months" CH 13)
10= *ešrum* (*adi ešrīšu* "up to ten times" CH 8)
12= *šinšer* (*adi šinšerīšu* "up to twelve times" CH 5)
30= *šalāšā* (*adi šalāšīšu* "up to thirty times" CH 8)

6.20 Determinatives

Determinatives are logograms placed before or after other logograms to indicate the general class to which the object denoted by the logogram belongs. For example, the determinatve GIŠ (= *iṣum*) is placed before words indicating trees or items made of wood; DINGIR (= *ilum*) is placed before names of gods. The determinative is written as a logogram in the transliteration but in the normalization it is customary to write its Akkadian form in superscript. For example, GIŠ.GU.ZA is normalized ^{iṣ}*kussûm*. Note that the Akkadian form of the determinative is placed in the construct state.

6.21 Determinatives in the sign list

Determinatives can be found in the sign list in the third column. A sign or group of signs preceded by a determinative will be found in the fourth column of the sign list under the sign immediately following the determinative. For example, GIŠ.GU.ZA will be found in the fourth column sub GU (217), not sub GIŠ (112).

6.22 Sumerian loan words

Sumerian loan words can be detected in Akkadian: (a) by the presence of an _e_ vowel (#6.6); (b) by the doubling of the last consonant, e.g., GU.ZA = _kussûm_ 'seat', SUKKAL = _sukkallum_ 'vizier'; (c) by the contraction at the end of a word, e.g., GU.ZA = _kussûm_, IGI.SÁ = _igisûm_ 'gift'.

6.23 The negative ul

The negative _ul_ is used in main clauses, e.g., _ul_ _uššab_ "he shall not sit"; _lā_ (#3.11) is used in subordinate and conditional clauses (e.g., _lā_ _uktînšu_ [If] he has not convicted him), and to negate imperatives (e.g., _lā_ _tanaddašši_ "don't throw it down" Ish 23).

6.24 Auxiliary verb târu

The verb _târu_ 'to return' is often used as an auxiliary verb. In combination with another verb it means "to do again." For example, _ul_ _itârma_ _itti_ _dayyānī_ _ina_ _dīnim_ _ul_ _uššab_ "he shall never again sit with the judges in a law case."

6.25 Root exercise

What are the roots, conjugations, and tenses of the following?

(1) _īteni_ (2) _ušetbi_ (3) _ištakkan_ (4) _ileqqe_ (5) _irtedi_ (6) _išemme_ (7) _ūtaššar_ (8) _iššakkan_ (9) _uṣaḫḫir_ (10) _uttîr_

Chapter 7

THE CODE OF HAMMURAPI
Law Two

7.0 Law two

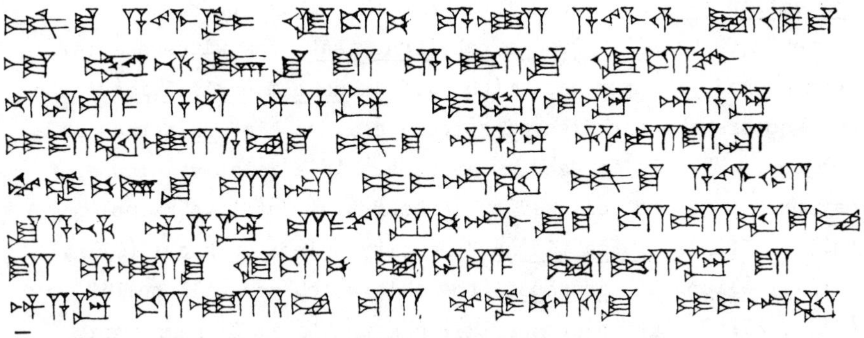

Transliterate and normalize the above using the basic sign list and the following additional signs not met with before:  lim (188 = ši)  DINGIR = ilum (10)  ÍD = Id (225)  É = bītum (127)  tab (61)

7.1 Vocabulary of law two

Nouns: kišpū '(charge of) sorcery', Id 'River god', bītum 'house', 'estate'.

Verbs: 'lk (alāku) I/1 (a, i) 'to go'

šl' (šalû) I/1 (i, i) 'to plunge'

kšd (kašādu) I/2 'to overcome'

tbl (tabālu) I/1 (a, a) 'to take away'

'bb (ebēbu) II/2 'to declare innocent'

šlm (šalāmu) I/2 'to be safe'

Preposition: ana 'unto'

7.2 The pronoun ša in relative clauses

In relative clauses the pronoun ša can serve as a subject 'who', object 'whom', genitive 'whose', or indirect object (preceded by a preposition), e.g., 'against whom', 'from whom', 'before whom', etc. When it serves as a genitive or indirect object ša must be followed by a resumptive pronominal suffix. Examples: ša elīšu kišpū nadû "the one against whom the charge was brought"; ša mimmûšu ḫalqu "whose property is lost" (CH 9); awīlum ša ḫulqum ina qātīšu ṣabtu "the man from whom the stolen property was seized" (CH 9); šībī ša ina maḫrišunu išām "the witnesses before whom he made the purchase (CH 9). In ša elīšu kišpī iddū "the one who brought a charge of sorcery against him" ša serves as a subject. When ša is used as an object in a relative clause it may or may not be followed by a resumptive suffix. Examples (with suffix): ālu ša tīdûšu "the city which you know: (Gilg. XI:11); elippu ša tabannūši "the ship which you will build" (Gilg. XI:28); (without suffix): dīnāt mīšarim ša Ḫammurapi šarrum lē'ûm ukinnu "the just laws which Hammurapi, the able king, established" (CH xxiv:1-5); ina Esagila ša arammu "in Esagila which I love" (CH xxiv:93-94).

7.3 The stative, and meanings of the tenses

The stative is the third of the Akkadian tenses (#1.11). Whereas the preterite usually denotes past time, e.g., iprus 'he cut', and the present indicates the present or future, e.g., iparras 'he cut', 'is cutting', 'will cut', the stative indicates a state of being, e.g., kabit 'it/he is/was heavy', damiq 'it/he is/was good'. In the I/1 conjugation the stative is the only tense in which some intransitive verbs like kabātu 'to be heavy' and damāqu 'to be good' occur. With transitive verbs the stative sometimes is used to indicate the passive. For example, ša elīšu kišpū nadû "the one against whom (the charge) of sorcery was brought."

7.4 Paradigm of the verb parāsu (a, u)

Singular	Preterite	Present	Stative
3rd masculine	iprus	iparras	paris
3rd feminine	iprus	iparras	parsat
2nd masculine	taprus	taparras	parsāta
2nd feminine	taprusī	taparrasī	parsāti
1st common	aprus	aparras	parsāku
Plural			
3rd masculine	iprusū	iparrasū	parsū
3rd feminine	iprusā	iparrasā	parsā
2nd masculine	taprusā	taparrasā	parsātunu
2nd feminine	taprusā	taparrasā	parsātina
1st common	niprus	niparras	parsānu

7.5 The conjugations

	Infinitive	Preterite	Present	Participle	Stative
I/1	parāsu	iprus	iparras	pārisu	paris
II/1	purrusu	uparris	uparras	muparrisu	purrus
III/1	šuprusu	ušapris	ušapras	mušaprisu	šuprus
IV/1	naprusu	ipparis	ipparras	mupparsu	naprus

7.6 Meanings of the conjugations

The I/1 expresses the basic meaning of the verb and corresponds to the Hebrew qal, the Arabic qatala, etc. Ihe II/1 modifies the meanings of the I/1 in a variety of ways. It corresponds to the Hebrew piʿel, the Arabic qattala, etc. The main function of the II/1 is to make verbs factitive (< Latin factitare 'to do often', 'to practice', 'to declare [someone] to be'). Examples: ebēbu I/1 'to be clean', 'to be pure', II/1 'to make clean', 'to declare pure or innocent' (ūtebbibaššu 'declared him innocent'); kânu I/1 'to be true/valid', II/1 'to prove', 'to convict'; lamādu I/1 'to learn', II/1 'to teach'; mašālu I/1 'to be equal', II/1 'to make equal'. Some verbs, however, only appear in the II conjugation, e.g., 'br (ebēru), II/1 'to accuse' (ubbir 'he accused' CH 1). The III/1 is mostly causative and corresponds to the Hebrew hiphʿil, the Arabic aqtala, etc. Examples: maqātu I/1 'to fall', III/1 'to cause to fall'; tebû I/1 'to get up', III/1 'to cause to get up', 'to remove'. The IV/1, which corresponds to the Hebrew niphʿal, serves as the passive for the I/1 conjugation, e.g., dâku I/1 'to kill', IV/1 'to be killed/executed' (iddâk 'he shall be executed').

7.7 The infixes

INFIXED T				INFIXED TAN	
	Preterite	Present		Preterite	Present
I/2	iptaras	iptarras	I/3	iptarras	iptanarras
II/2	uptarris	uptarras	II/3	uptarris	uptanarras
III/2	uštapris	uštapras	III/3	uštapris	uštanapras
IV/2	ittapras		IV/3	ittapras	ittanapras

7.8 Meanings of the infixes

Many times the exact meaning of the infixes is unknown, e.g., in uktîn in CH 1, or in ittanašši in CH 5. Generally the I/2 has reflexive or reciprocal (expressing mutual relation) meaning. Examples: išriq 'he stole', ištariq 'he stole for himself'; imḫaṣ 'he struck', imtaḫaṣ 'he struck others' = 'he fought'. The I/3 normally gives the root an iterative (frequentative) or habitual connotation, e.g., kašādu 'to arrive', iktaššad 'he used to arrive'; šakānu 'to put', ištanakkan 'he will continually put'.

7.9 The determinative DINGIR

The determinative DINGIR is used before names of deities. In the normalization it is customary to write it with a small *d* in superscript instead of using the construct of *ilum* (#6.20), e.g., ^{d}*Marduk*, ^{d}*Šamaš*, ^{d}*Id*.

7.10 Assimilation of consonants

As has already been observed in the case of an *n* at the end of a syllable (#2.3) certain consonants assimilate into other consonants. Two further assimilations encountered in law two are: (a) the *m* of ventive *am* assimilates into the following consonant, e.g., *ūtebbibamšūma* > *ūtebbibaššūma*; (b) when the third person suffixes (e.g., *šu* or *šunu*) are attached to sibilants or dentals both the *š* of the suffix and the sibilant or dental goes to *s*. Examples: *iktašadšu* > *iktašassu*; *bītšu* > *bissu*.

7.11 Asyndetic clause

Asyndeton occurs when conjunctions are omitted between clauses. In Akkadian this normally means the omission of the enclitic *ma* (#3.9). For example, *ša elīšu kišpī iddû iddâk ša* ^{d}*Id išli'am bīt mubbirīšu itabbal* "the one who brought (a charge of) sorcery against him will be executed, while the one who plunged into the River will take away the estate of his accuser."

7.12 Ventive in a relative clause

In a relative clause the ventive (#4.11) does not take the subjunctive *u* which would normally be expected after *ša* (#4.15). For example, *ša* ^{d}*Id išli'am* "the one who plunged into the River."

7.13 Noun suffixes

The pronominal suffixes to the noun are:

	Singular	Plural
1st common	ī/ya/'a	ni
2nd masculine	ka	kunu
2nd feminine	ki	kina
3rd masculine	šu	šunu
3rd feminine	ša	šina

7.14 Attachment of suffixes to the noun

The suffixes are attached according to the case of the noun. In the genitive case the suffixes are attached to the genitive form of the noun, e.g., ana šarrīšu 'to his king', bīt mubbirīšu 'the estate of his accuser'. Note the lengthening of the i vowel when the suffixes are attached (otherwise it would drop out according to rule six #2.8). In the nominative and accusative cases the form of the noun before suffixes will depend on how the noun forms its construct (#4.8).

A. If a noun forms its construct by dropping case endings (#4.9) the suffixes are attached to the construct form, e.g., bēlšu 'his lord', bītka 'your house', waradka 'your slave', uzunša 'her ear', mubbiršu 'his accuser'.

B. If a noun forms its construct by using the genitive form (#4.10) the suffixes are attached to the regular nominative and accusative case endings without the mimation. Examples:

	Construct	Nominative	Accusative
abum	abi	abu + šu	aba + šu
mimmûm	mimmî	mimmû + šu	mimmâ + šu
šarrū	šarrī	šarrū + šu	šarrī + šu

C. Note, however, that geminates (#4.9B) and some feminine nouns have suffixes attached to the accusative form for both the nominative and accusative cases. Examples:

	Nominative	Accusative
libbum	libbašu	libbašu
šarrum	šarrašu	šarrašu
alaktum	alaktašu	alaktašu

Chapter 8

THE CODE OF HAMMURAPI
Laws Six - Eight

8.0 Laws six - eight

Law six

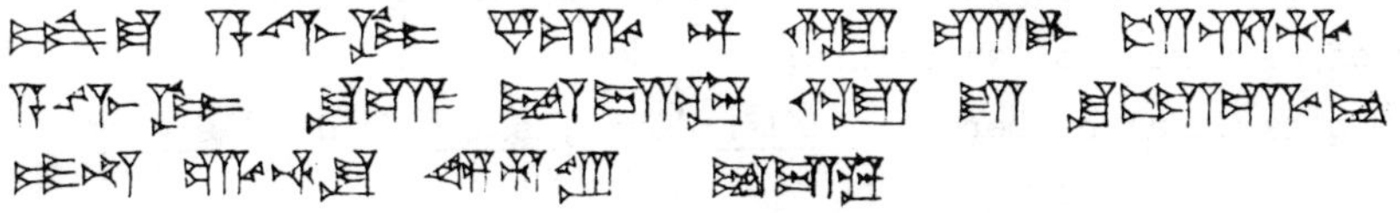

Law seven

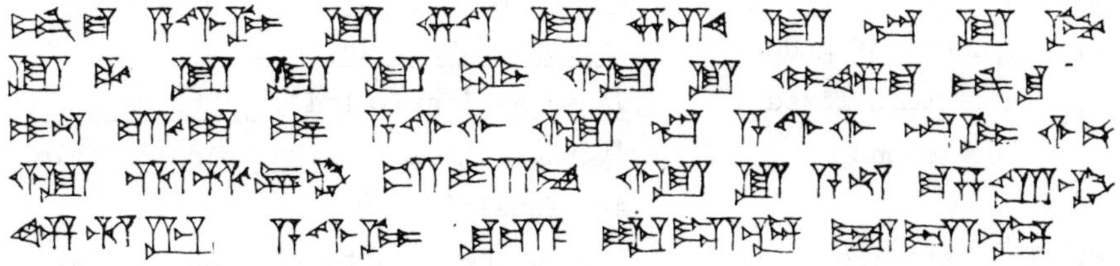

Law eight

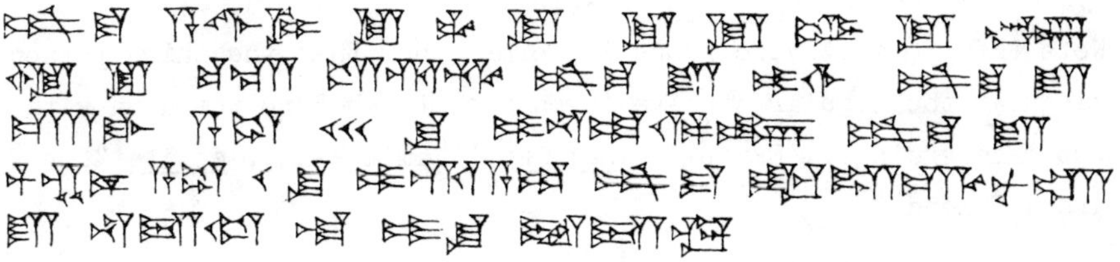

Transliterate, normalize, and analyze the above using the sign list and the glossary.

8.1 The coordinating conjunction lū...lū

In a series lū...lū are employed to express 'either...or'. In a series of three or more alternatives the final lū is normally preceded by u. For example, lū kaspam lū ḫurāṣam lū wardam lū amtam...u lū mimma šumšu "either silver, gold, a slave, a female slave...or anything whatsoever."

8.2 Indefinite pronoun mimma

The indefinite pronoun mimma 'whatever' is indeclinable. With šumšu 'its name' it becomes an idiom for 'everything whatsoever', e.g., u lū mimma šumšu "or anything whatsoever."

8.3 The status absolutus

The status absolutus is a form of the noun without case endings and is very similar to the construct. It is employed in a variety of ways some of which are:

A.	In cardinal numbers	ištēn 'one', šalāš 'three' šinšer 'twelve'
B.	In measures	mana 'mina', šiqil 'shekel'
C.	In vocatives	šar 'O king', bēl 'O lord'
D.	In names of gods	Marduk, Šamaš, Id, Bēl
E.	In certain fixed expressions	lā šanān 'unrivaled', ṣeḫer rabi 'young and old', zikar sinniš 'male and female'
F.	To stativize a noun	šarrāq "he is a thief" (CH 7), šar "he is a liar" (CH 11), aššat "she is a wife"

Note that to stativize nouns in forms other than the third person singular the regular stative forms are attached to the noun without case endings. Examples: šarrāku "I am a king", ebrāta "You are a friend."

8.4 Disjunctive sentences

In disjunctive clauses (clauses setting two or more expressions in opposition to each other) the conjunction šumma (#3.2) is used with one or more šumma's to indicate "if...or if". For example, šumma ša ilim šumma ša ēkallim "If it belongs to the god or if it belongs to the palace."

8.5 The pronoun ša as a genitive indicator

The pronoun ša (#6.16) can be used as a genitive indicator expressing 'the one of' or 'that of'. It is also used to denote possession, e.g., ša ilim "that of the god", "belonging to the god"; ša ēkallim "that of the palace", "belonging to the palace". The expression ša nadānim "that of paying" means "the amount necessary for payment."

8.6 Infixed ān

In some nouns an infixed ān occurs before the case ending. Its effect is to give the noun a particularizing meaning. Examples: šarrāqum 'a thief', šarrāqānum 'a thief in a particular theft' = 'that thief'; nādinum 'a seller', nādinānum 'a seller in a particular transaction' = 'that seller'.

8.7 The verb išû

The verb išû 'to have' is found only in the preterite and stative tenses. For the present tense the verb rašû is used, e.g., iraššì 'he will have'. The earliest form of the preterite is īšu which later becomes īši.

8.8 The form irī'ab

The form irī'ab comes from the verb râbu (a, i) 'to compensate' and is a I/1 present. The middle consonant, which has dropped (#2.1), was originally y (yod), so the real root letters are ryb. Substituting ryb into the paradigm form iparras (#2.2) we get irayyab which goes to irīyab (rule three, #2.5), but does not go according to rule four (#2.6) to irâb (see #4.14 on uncontracted verbs in OB). However, instead of irīyab this form is written in the text i-ri-a-ab, and in conformity with our system of inserting an ' (aleph) sign between two uncontracted vowels (#4.14) we normalize the form irī'ab.

Chapter 9

THE CODE OF HAMMURAPI
Laws Nine - Thirteen

9.0 Laws nine - thirteen

Law nine

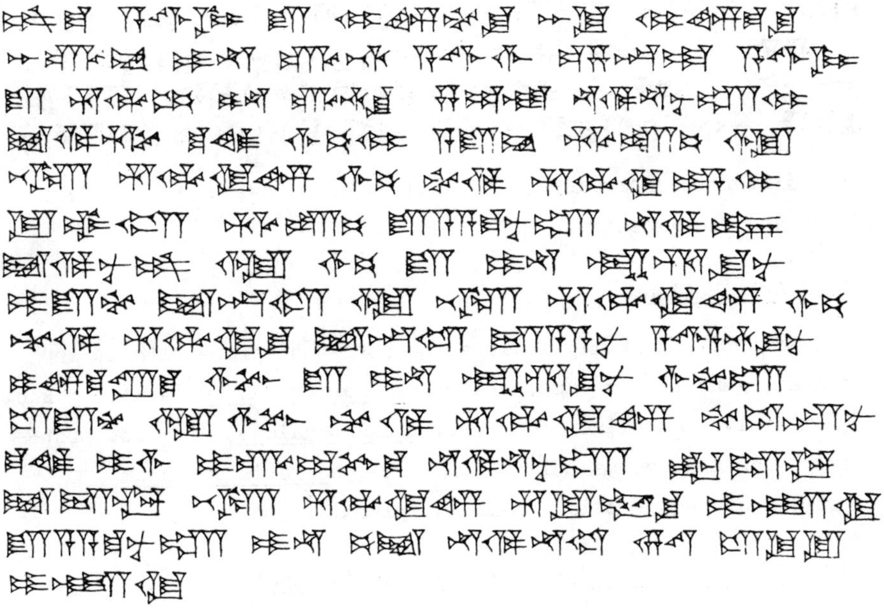

Law ten

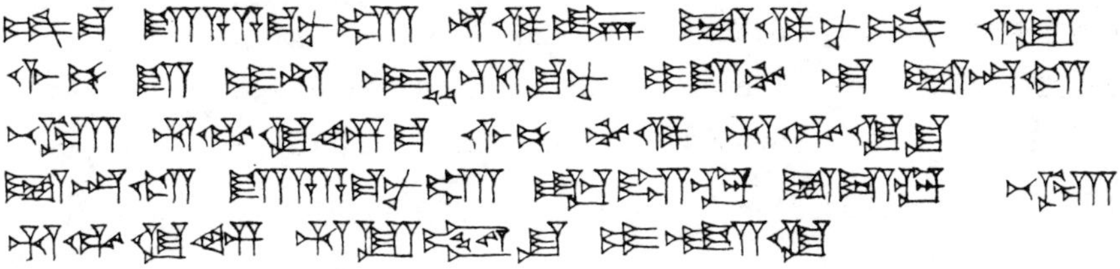

Law eleven

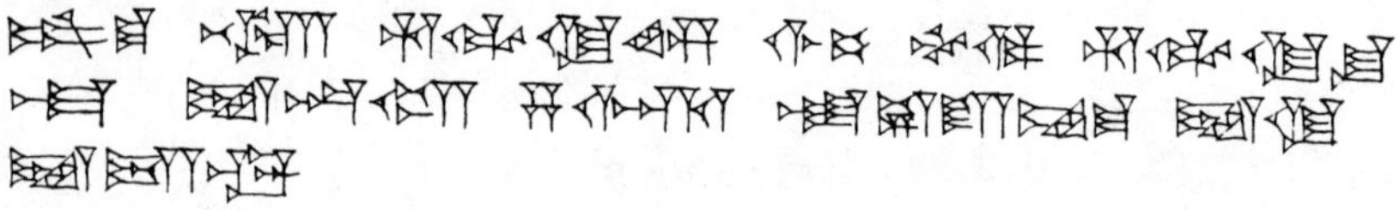

Law twelve

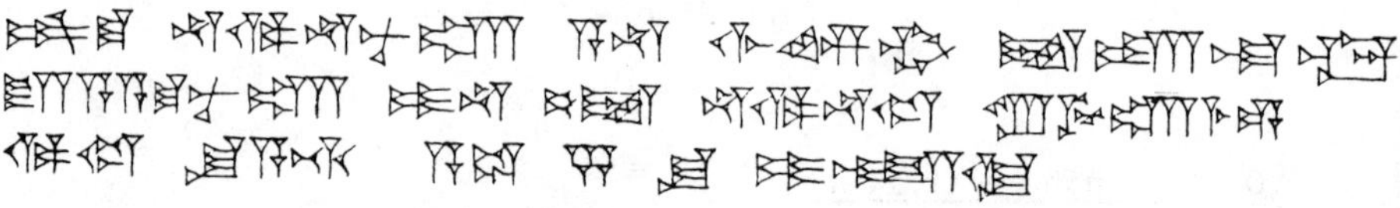

Law thirteen

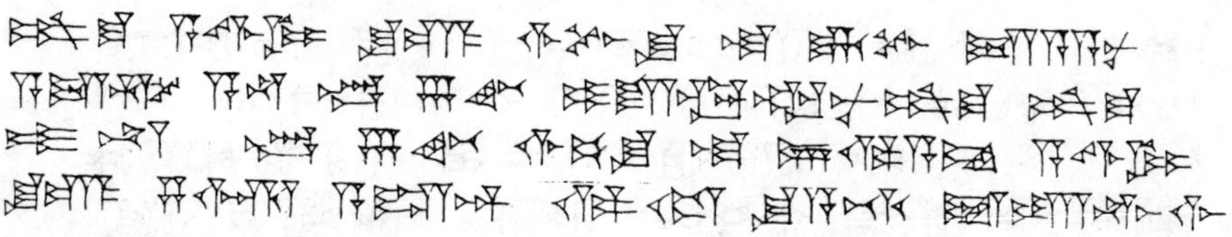

Transliterate, normalize, and analyze the above using the sign list and the glossary.

9.1 Attribution

The adjective normally follows the noun and agrees with it in number, gender, and case. Examples: <u>šarrum</u> <u>dannum</u> 'a strong king' (nominative masculine singular), <u>mimmâšu</u> <u>ḫalqam</u> 'his lost property' (accusative masculine singular), <u>šarrātim</u> <u>dannātim</u> 'strong queens' (oblique feminine plural).

9.2 Paradigm of the adjective dannum 'strong'

	Masculine		Feminine	
	Singular	Plural	Singular	Plural
Nominative	dannum	dannūtum	dannatum	dannātum
Accusative	dannam	dannūtim	dannatam	dannātim
Genitive	dannim	dannūtim	dannatim	dannātim

This paradigm should be compared with that of the noun in #3.4.

It will be noted that the main difference in forms between the noun and the adjective is in the masculine plural. The noun forms are šarrū, šarrī, šarrī, while the adjective forms are dannūtum, dannūtim, dannūtim. Examples: šarrū dannūtum 'strong kings' (nominative); wardī damqūtim 'good slaves' (oblique).

9.3 Assimilation of consonants II (see #7.10)

An infixed t in verbs with initial ṣ, ṭ, or z will produce the following changes: ṣt > ṣṣ; ṭt > ṭṭ; zt > zz. Examples: iṣtabat > iṣṣabat; iṭtarad > iṭṭarad (CH 26); iztakar > izzakar (CH 18).

9.4 The particle mi

The particle mi indicates that the clause in which it is found is a direct quotation. It has no fixed position and can be placed anywhere within the clause. Examples: nādinānummi iddinam "that seller sold it to me"; maḫar šībīmi ašām "I bought (it) before witnesses"; šībī mūdê ḫulqīyāmi lublam "let me bring witnesses who know my lost property." Note the lengthening of the vowel when mi is attached, cf., #3.9.

9.5 The precative

The precative expresses a wish or desire. It is formed with the particle lū and the preterite, e.g., lū taprus 'may you cut', lū nišme 'let us hear'. In the 1st person singular and the 3rd person singular and plural lū and the preterite are joined together, e.g., lū + aprus > luprus, lū + iprus > liprus, lū + iprusū > liprusū, lū + ublam > lublam "let me bring here."

9.6 Verbal suffixes

The suffixes which are attached to the verb are different from those attached to the noun (#7.13). Verbal suffixes may be direct (accusative), or indirect (dative). The direct suffix šu was met in forms such as uktînšu "he has convicted him" (CH 1), ušetbūšu "they shall remove him" (CH 5). The indirect suffix for the 3rd masculine singular is šum, e.g., nādin iddinūšum "the seller who sold to him." The full paradigm of the suffixes is as follows:

	DIRECT SUFFIXES		INDIRECT SUFFIXES	
	Singular	Plural	Singular	Plural
1st common	ni	ni'āti	am/nim	ni'āšim
2nd masculine	ka	kunūti	kum	kunūšim
2nd feminine	ki	kināti	kim	kināšim
3rd masculine	šu	šunūti	šum	šunūšum
3rd feminine	ši	šināti	šim	šināšim

Note that the indirect suffixes are often attached to the ventive am (#4.11), e.g., iprusam + šum > iprusaššum (#7.10a), petašši < (petâm + ši) "open for her" (Ish 38).

9.7 The IV/1 preterite of šâmu

The IV/1 preterite form of middle weak verbs with original aleph is ipparas (not ipparis, #7.5). For example, the IV/1 preterite of š'm (šâmu) 'to buy' is iššâm, e.g., šībū ša ina maḫrīšunu šīmum iššâmu "the witnesses before whom the purchase was made."

9.8 The idiom ana šimtim alāku

The idiom ana šimtim alāku (literally "to go to one's fate") is a euphemism for 'to die'. For example, šumma nādinānum ana šimtim ittalak "If that seller has died."

9.9 Casus pendens in the nominative

The casus pendens is normally found in the oblique case (#6.11). A departure from the norm is šumma awīlum šû šībūšu lā qerbū "If, as for that man, his witnesses are not at hand."

9.10 The determinative KAM

The determinative kam (165) is used after numerals and is not indicated in the normalization. For example, ana ITU.ÀŠ.KAM = ana šeššet warḫī "up to six months."

9.11 Polarity of numerals

Akkadian has a masculine and feminine form of the numerals. As in the other Semitic languages polarity is observed (in Akkadian from three through nineteen), that is, a number will appear with a noun of the opposite gender. Thus a masculine form of the number will occur with a feminine noun and a feminine form of the number with a masculine noun. For example, in ana šeššet warḫī "up to six months" the feminine form of the numeral is used with the masculine noun warḫum 'month'.

Chapter 10

THE CODE OF HAMMURAPI
Laws Fourteen - Twenty-two

10.0 Laws fourteen - twenty-two

Law fourteen

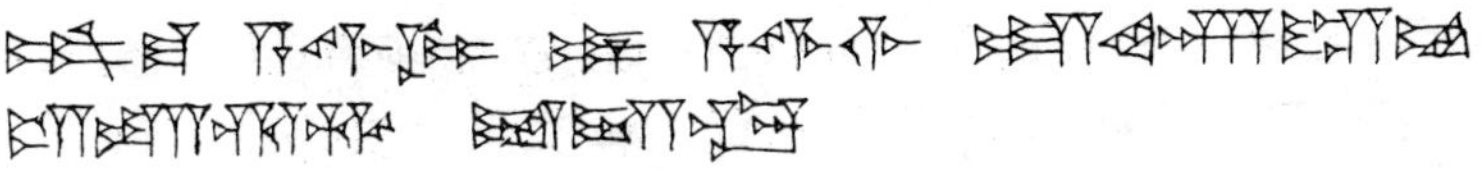

Law fifteen

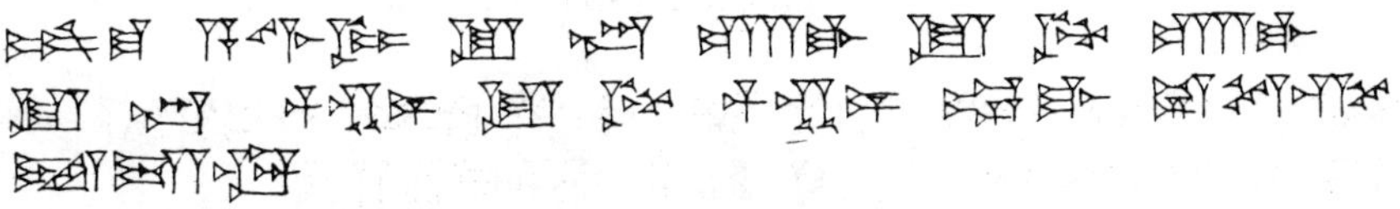

Law sixteen

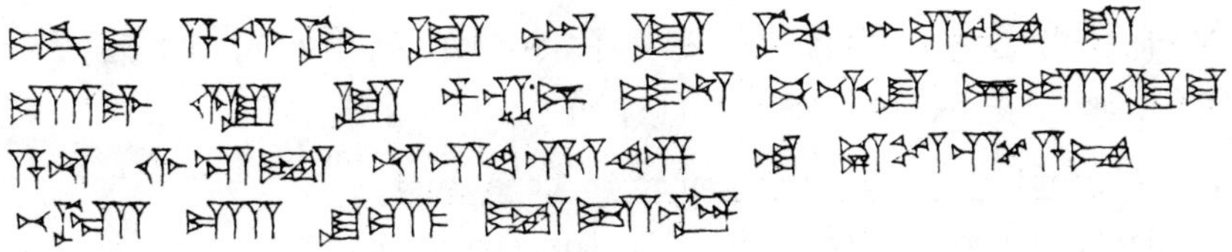

Law seventeen

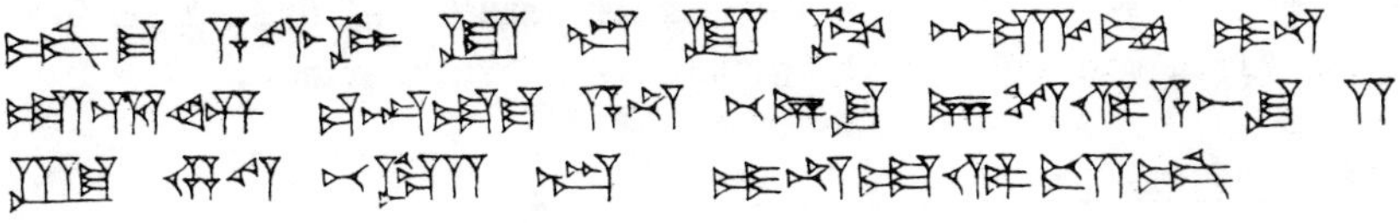

Law eighteen

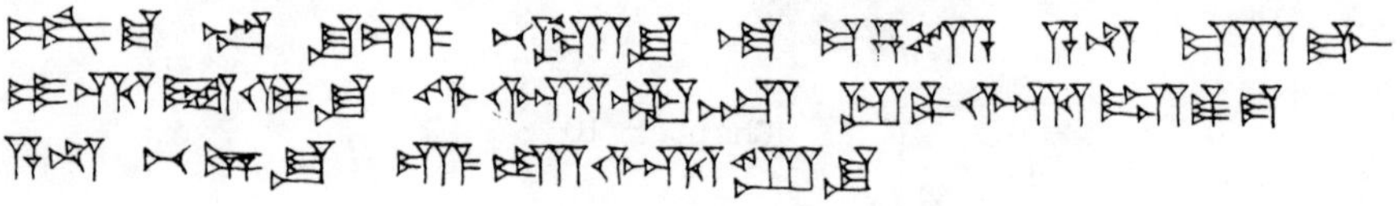

Law nineteen

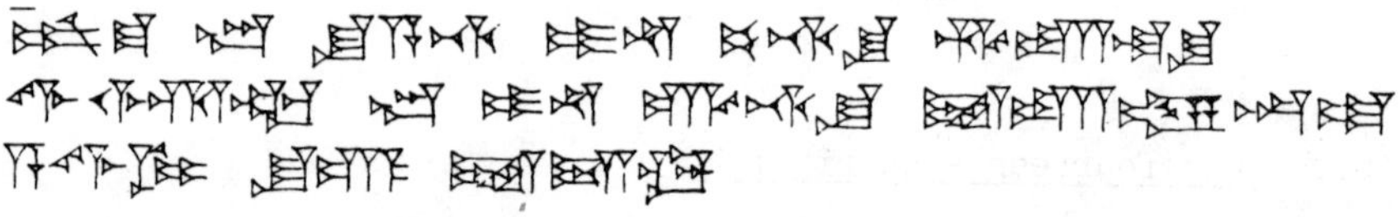

Law twenty

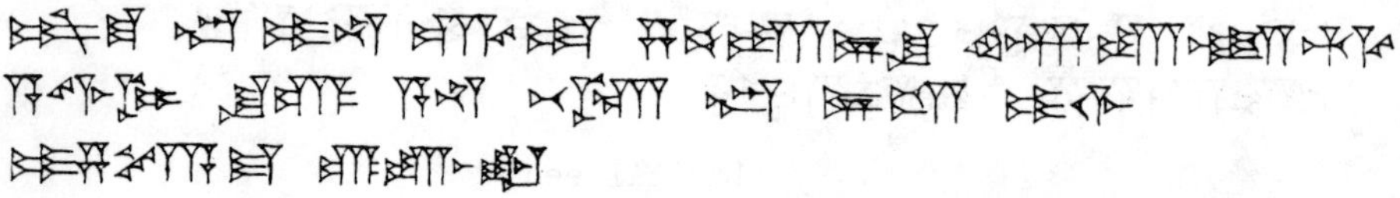

Law twenty-one

Law twenty-two

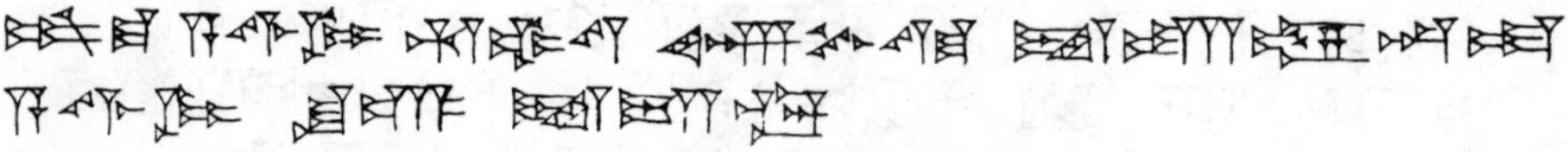

10.1 Adjective qualifying nouns in construct

An adjective qualifying a noun in the construct of a construct-genitive phrase is placed in the case the noun would be were it not in this phrase. For example, šumma awīlum mār awīlim ṣeḫram ištariq "If a man kidnaps the young son of another man."

10.2 Accusative of specification

When the accusative is used to indicate an adverbial or prepositional phrase absent from the text it is called the accusative of specification. The accusative of specification thus answers the "when", "where", or "how" demanded by the context. For example, abullam uštēṣi "He let him escape through the city gate."

10.3 The III conjugation of initial w verbs

The expected III/1 form of initial w verbs (e.g., wašābu) is ušūšib (< ušawšib, rule three #2.5). However, forms such as ušāšib and ušēšib are also found. Some initial w verbs (like wašābu) exhibit all three forms, others only one or two. Examples: from wabālu, ušābil, ušēbil; from waṣû, ušūṣi, ušēṣi, uštēṣi.

10.4 Adjective qualifying several nouns

An adjective qualifying several nouns usually stands after the last one in the series. Where there is a difference of gender among the nouns the adjective concurs with the masculine. For example, lū wardam lū amtam ḫalqam "either a fugitive male slave or a fugitive female slave."

10.5 Use of ša instead of construct-genitive

The pronoun ša as genitive indicator (#8.5) is used instead of the construct-genitive for greater clarity where the latter might be confusing because of there being a number of nouns, or because one or both parts of the construct-genitive phrase needs to be qualified by adjectives. For example, lū wardam lū amtam ḫalqam ša ēkallim "either a fugitive male slave or a fugitive female slave belonging to the palace."

10.6 Case of the measured item

While the measure itself is placed in the status absolutus (#8.3B) the thing measured is put in the case it would be were there no measure involved. For example, KÙ.BABBAR is normalized as kaspam (accusative) in šinā šiqil kaspam bēl wardim inaddiššum "the owner of the slave shall give to him two shekels of silver."

10.7 The idiom nīš ilim zakāru

The idiom nīš ilim zakāru (literally "to mention the life of the god") is used primarily in oaths and means 'to swear', 'to take an oath'. For example, awīlum šû ana bēl wardim nīš ilim izakkar "that man shall swear to the owner of the slave."

10.8 Thematic vowel of the I/1 present of middle weak verbs

In the I/1 conjugation of middle weak verbs the thematic vowel of the present is identical to that of the preterite when vocalic affixes are added. Examples: the I/1 3rd person plural present of kânu is ikunnū (not ikânu or ikannū, #6.15), the preterite is ikūnū; the I/1 3rd person plural present of dâku is idukkū, the preterite is idūkū; Ihe I/1 present of nâḫu with subjunctive is inuḫḫu (Ish 96).

Chapter 11

THE CODE OF HAMMURAPI
Laws Twenty-three - Twenty-nine

11.0 Laws twenty-three - twenty-nine

Law twenty-three

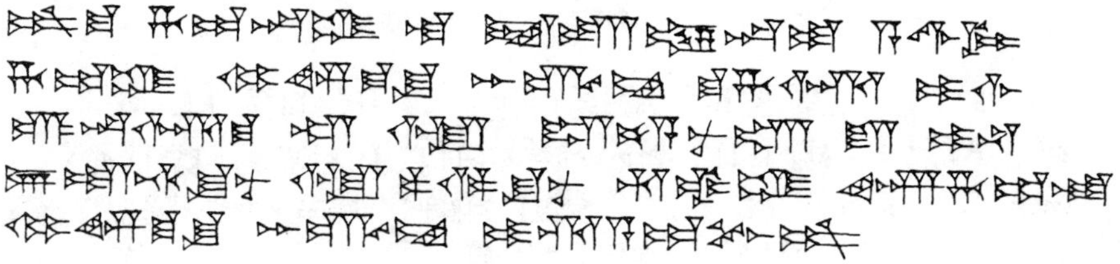

Law twenty-four

Law twenty-five

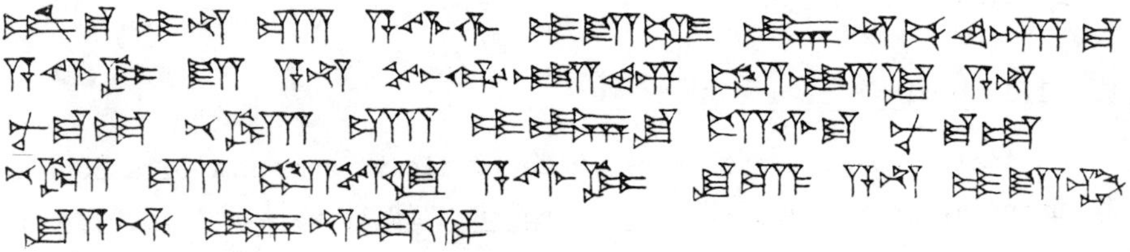

Law twenty-six

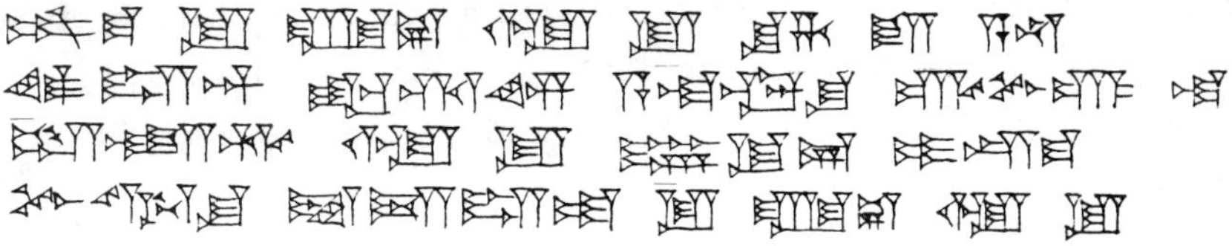

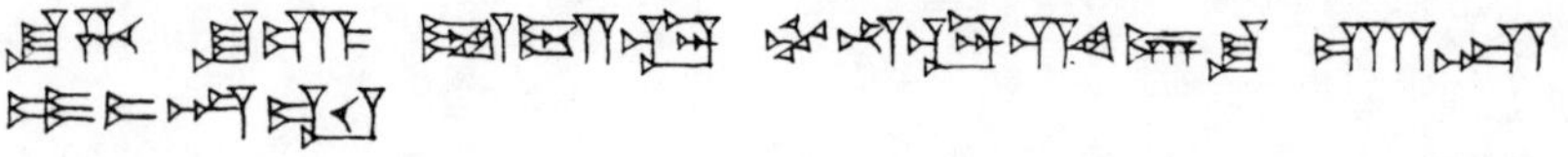

Law twenty-seven

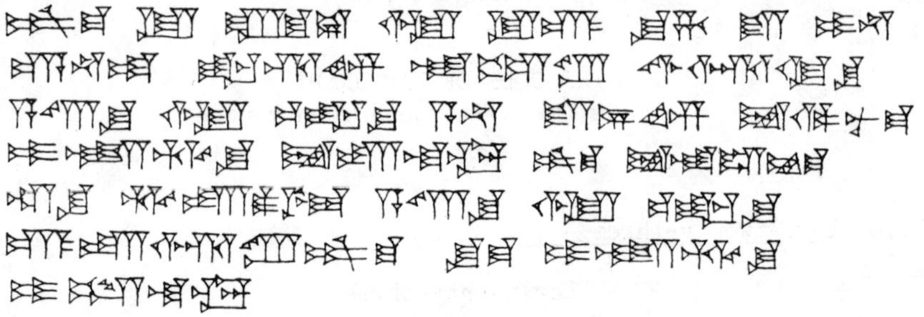

Law twenty-eight

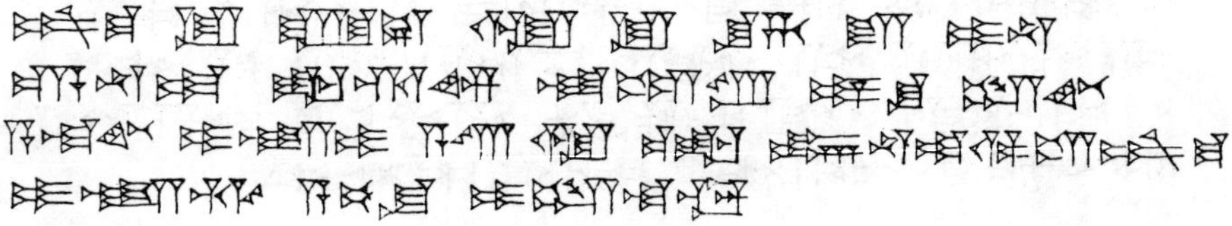

Law twenty-nine

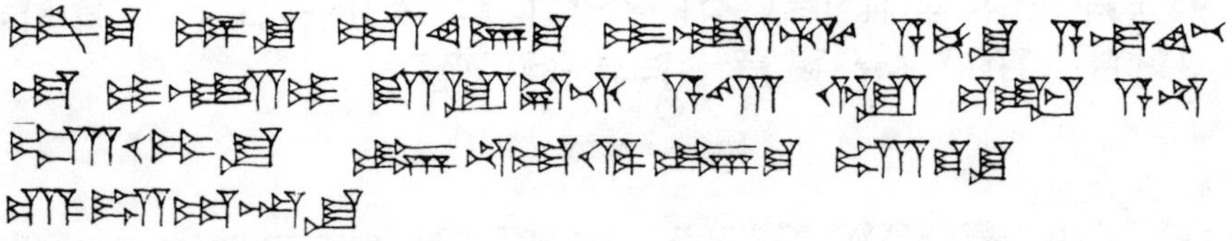

11.1 Nominal clause

Nominal clauses are clauses whose predicate consists of a noun or pronoun. For example, <u>šumma</u> <u>napištum</u> "If it were a life."

11.2 The 3rd person feminine singular

In Old Babylonian (OB) there is no special form for the preterite or present of the third person feminine singular. Thus <u>iprus</u> means 'he cut' or 'she cut'. For example, <u>išātum</u> <u>innapiḫ</u> "fire broke out."

11.3 Infinitive used as a noun

The infinitive is properly a verbal noun, that is, a noun which can be construed verbally. As a noun it can be declined (#6.12) or have suffixes attached. For example, alākšu qabû "his going out was commanded."

11.4 The form warkīšu in CH 27

The force of the suffix attached to the preposition warki 'after' is as a resumptive pronominal suffix to a casus pendens (#6.11). Thus šumma lū rēdâm u lū bā'iram ša ina dannat šarrim turru warkīšu, literally, "If, as for a rēdûm-soldier or a bā'irum-soldier who was captured in the king's fortress, after him..." may be rendered "If, after a rēdûm-soldier or a bā'irum-soldier was captured in the king's fortress, (his field or orchard was given to another who performed the corvée work, now if he returned and reached his city, his field or orchard shall be returned to him, and he himself will perform the corvée work)."

11.5 Enclitic ma used for emphasis

As well as serving to connect clauses (#3.9) enclitic ma is used to emphasize a word. For example, šûma ilikšu illak "He himself will perform the corvée work."

11.6 Infinitive in the accusative

Certain verbs require a preceding infinitive to be placed in the accusative. These are generally verbs of command (e.g., qabû), or capability (e.g., le'û). For example, ilkam alākam ilî "he is able to perform the corvée work."

11.7 The IV/1 present of nadānu

The IV/1 present of nadānu 'to give' is innaddin (not innaddan according to the paradigm ipparras, #7.5). For example, eqlum u kirûm innaddiššum "the field or orchard shall be given to him."

Chapter 12

THE DESCENT OF ISHTAR
Lines 1-11

12.0 The Descent of Ishtar lines 1-11

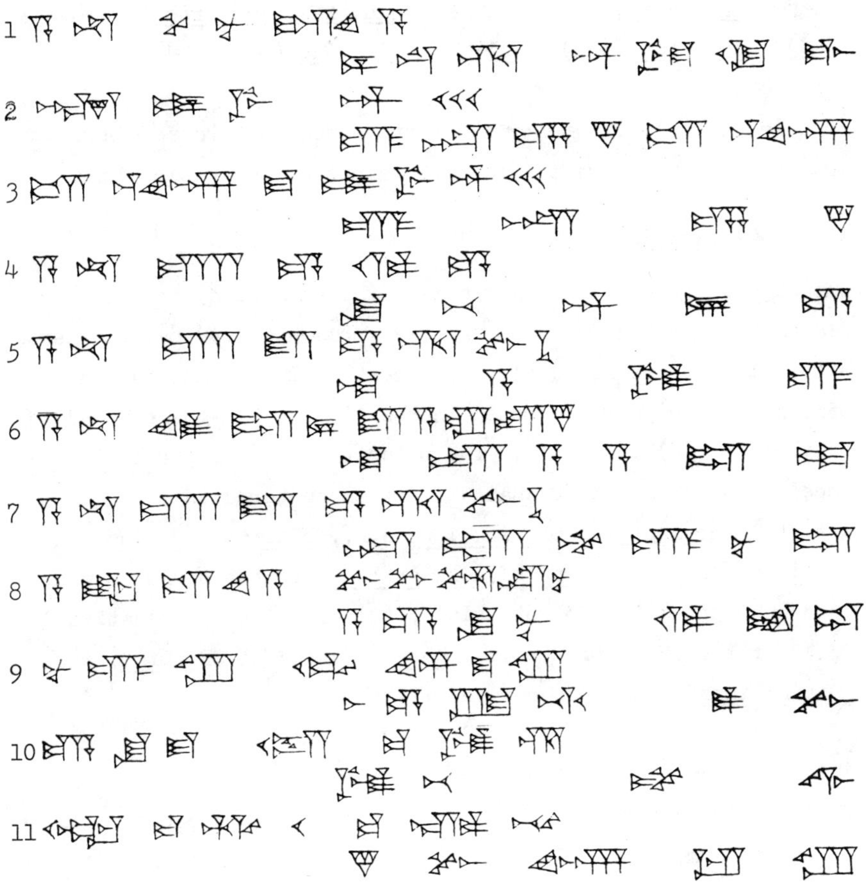

12.1 Polyphonous basic signs

As will have already been noticed a number of the basic signs are polyphonous (#2.17). Some of the common polyphonous values which appear in the Descent of Ishtar are:

be = bat, til (29) du = kup (94) ud = per, tam (159) ri = dal (44) ur = lik, taš (224) ši = lim (188) me = šib (206)

12.2 Other polyphonous signs

Other common (though non-basic) polyphonous signs which occur in the Descent of Ishtar are:

ḫar, mur (171) dan, kal, lab, reb (125) lak, rid (121) riš, šak (58) qer, biš (142)

Because of their frequency it is suggested that these signs be learnt along with the polyphonous values of the basic signs.

12.3 Standard Babylonian (SB)

Although written in the same script (Neo-Assyrian) in which the Old Babylonian Code of Hammurapi was presented (#0.6), the texts with which we are now dealing (Descent of Ishtar and the Annals of Sennacherib) were composed in the literary language Standard Babylonian (SB), cf. #0.4. The principal morphological differences between OB and SB that will be encountered in these texts are: (1) the dropping of mimation, e.g., bīti and šu (instead of OB bītim and šum) in ana bīti ša ēribūšu "to the house to which those who enter it (do not exit)"; (2) use of the nominative form or the accusative, e.g., nūru (instead of OB nūram) in nūru ul immarū "they do not see light."

12.4 The writing of Ištar and Sin in line 2

The sign for Ištar is written as a ligature consisting of the determinative sign (10) and the Ištar sign

(51). The god Sin is written with the numeral 30 𒌍 (199) to indicate that Sin, the moon god, is literally the god of thirty (days).

12.5 The phrase uzna šakānu

The phrase *uzna šakānu* (literally, "to set the ear") means "to direct one's attention." For example, *iškunma mārat* ^{d}*Sîn uzunša* "The daughter of Sin directed her attention (to the dark house)."

12.6 Declension of the participle

The participle is declined as a noun, e.g., masculine singular *pārisu*, masculine plural *pārisū*, feminine singular *pāristu*, feminine plural *pārisātu*. Examples of the masculine plural participle are *ēribū* "those who enter" and *āṣû* "those who exit."

12.7 Loss of initial w

After OB times a *w* at the beginning of a word will drop out, e.g., *wāṣû* > *āṣû*, *wašbū* > *ašbū*, *wardātim* > *ardāti* (line 35), *warki* > *arki* (line 76).

12.8 Active meanings of the stative

One of the most common functions of the stative (#7.3) is to describe the subject especially the subject's appearance, posture, and position. For example, what he wears (*labiš*), or the fact that he is sitting (*ašib*). Thus the stative will frequently have an active meaning. Examples: *ana ḫarrāni ša alaktaša lā tārat* "to the road whose course does not turn back"; *nūru ul immarū ina eṭûti ašbū* "they do not see light, they dwell in darkness."

12.9 The subjunctive on stative forms

Except for the 3rd person masculine singular the subjunctive is not indicated when it occurs with stative forms. For example, *ana ḫarrāni ša alaktaša lā tārat* "to the road whose course does not turn back."

12.10 The conjunction *ašar*

The conjunction *ašar* means 'where'. Note that although the form *ašar* is a construct (< *ašru* 'place') the noun which follows is not in the genitive. For example, *ašar epru bubussunu* "where dust is their food."

12.11 Statives of the *paras* and *parus* type

As well as the more normal *paris* form, the stative can also have forms *paras* and *parus*. Examples: *rapaš* 'is wide', *maruṣ* 'is sick', *šabuḫ* 'is poured'.

Chapter 13

THE DESCENT OF ISHTAR
Lines 12-18

13.0 The Descent of Ishtar lines 12-18

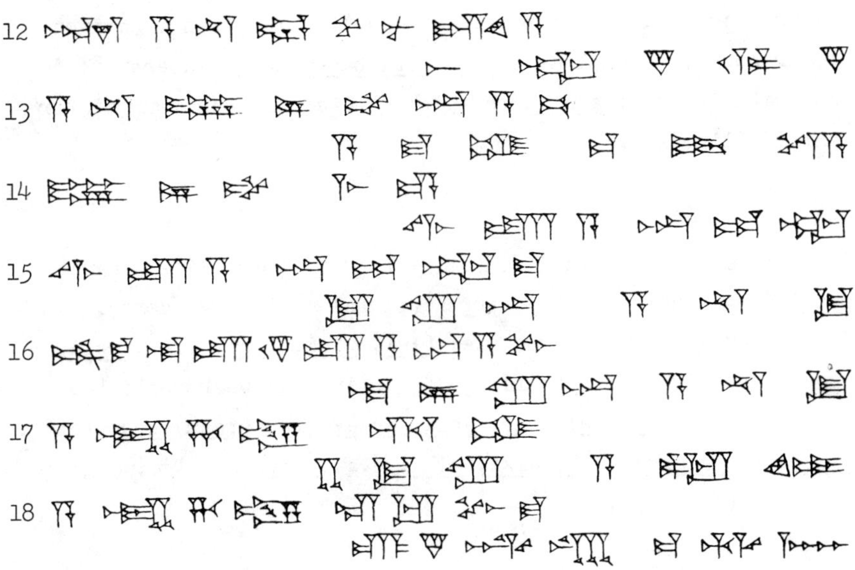

13.1 Infinitive with ina

The infinitive with *ina* serves as a temporal clause. For example, *ina kašād bēlīya* "when my lord arrives." When the subject precedes the infinitive takes a resumptive pronominal suffix. Examples: ^{d}*Ištar ana bāb erṣet lā târi ina kašādīša* "when Ishtar arrived at the gate of the netherworld"; ^{d}*Ereškigal annîta ina šemîša* "when Ereshkigal heard this" (line 28).

13.2 Mimation in SB

Mimation, which normally would not be expected after OB times (#12.3), is retained occasionally in SB. For example, amatum izzakkar. Furthermore, mimation returns before enclitic ma, e.g., ištu ullânumma 'ever since' (line 63).

13.3 The vocative

The status absolutus (#8.3C) is used for the vocative. For example, ātî mē petâ bābka "O gatekeeper, open your gate for me."

13.4 The particle mē

The form mē is a poetic particle used to strengthen vocatives and pronouns. Examples: ātî mē petâ bābka "O gatekeeper, open your gate for me"; annītu mē aḫātki dIštar "Behold your sister Ishtar" (line 26).

13.5 The imperative

The imperative is formed as follows: purus (masculine singular), pursī (feminine singular), pursā (plural of both genders). In final weak verbs the forms are: bini, binî, binâ, e.g., petâ (peti + ventive a) "open for me." In initial weak verbs the forms are: (for aḫāzu) aḫuz, aḫzī, aḫzā; (for epēšu) epuš, epšī, epšā; (for alāku) alik, alkī, alkā, e.g., alik ātî "go, O gatekeeper!" (line 37).

13.6 The precative with initial weak verbs

For the precative with the 1st person singular and 3rd person singular and plural, see #9.5. When the precative lū is attached to initial weak verbs it will have a macron. Thus lū + ēruba = lūruba "that I can enter here"; lū + īkul = līkul "let him eat." Note that there is no macron on lullik (line 24) because of the double consonant (#2.7).

13.7 Independent pronouns

The independent pronoun has three cases: nominative, genitive/ accusative, and dative (#5.8). The full declension is as follows:

Nominative	Genitive/Accusative		Dative	
anāku	yâti		yâši	
attā	kâti/a		kâši/a	
attī	kâti		kâši	
šû	šu'āti/u	šâti/u	šu'āši	šâši/a/u
šî	ši'āti	šâti	ši'āsi	šâši/a
nīnu	ni'āti	nâti	ni'āši	nâši
attunu	kunūti		kunūši	
attina	kināti		kināši	
šunu	šunūti		šunūši	
šina	šināti		šināši	

Note that the independent pronouns can be used for emphasis, e.g., lūruba anāku, literally, "so that I can enter here, I."

13.8 Purpose clause after an imperative

The imperative is often followed by a precative indicating a purpose or final clause. For example, petâ bābkāma lūruba anāku "Open the gate for me so that I can enter here." In these cases a ma frequently precedes the precative clause.

13.9 Trochaeus in epic texts

Epic texts (like the Descent of Ishtar) tend to have trochaic meter, especially at the end of a line. For example,

ātî mē petâ bā́bka
petâ bābkāma lūruba anā́ku

13.10 Purpose clause after šumma

A purpose clause following a šumma protasis is placed in the same tense as the šumma clause. For example, šumma lā tapattâ bābu lā erruba anāku "If you won't open the gate for me so that I cannot enter here."

13.11 The present tense after šumma

After the conjunction šumma a verb in the present tense indicates: (a) volition, intention, or wishing; (b) habitualness; (c) simple future. Examples of (a) are: šumma awīlum ḫirtašu ša mārū lā uldušum izzib "if a man wishes to divorce his wife who did not bear him children" (CH 138); šumma lā tapattâ bābu lā erruba anāku "if you won't open the gate for me so that I cannot enter here."

13.12 Quadriliteral verbs

The two main groups of quadriliteral verbs are represented by the verbs šuḫarruru 'to be quiet', 'to cease' and nabalkutu 'to overturn', 'to remove'.

13.13 The šuḫarruru type

The šuḫarruru type has a š as the first letter and is similar to the II stem. It forms its preterite ušḫarrir, and its present ušḫarrar. For example, inūḫ tâmtu ušḫarrirma imḫullu abūbu iklu "The sea became calm, the storm abated, the flood ceased" (Gilgamesh XI:131). Other verbs of this type are šuparruru 'to spread out', šuqallulu 'to suspend', šuqammumu 'to be silent'.

13.14 The nabalkutu type

The nabalkutu type has an n as the first letter and a l or r as the second root letter. This type forms both a I (similar to the regular IV) and III conjugation.

	Preterite	Present
I/1	ibbalkit	ibbalakkat
III/1	ušbalkit ušabalkit	ušbalakkat ušbalkat ušabalkat

For example, amaḫḫaṣ sippūma ušabalkat dalāti "I will smite the door-jambs and remove the door." Other verbs of this type are _naparqudu_ 'to fall or lie on one's back', _naparšudu_ 'to escape', _napalkû_ 'to be wide', _neperdû_ 'to be bright', _negeltû_ 'to awake', _nekelmû_ 'to look at (in a malevolent sense)' etc.

Chapter 14

THE DESCENT OF ISHTAR
Lines 19-30

14.0 The Descent of Ishtar lines 19-30

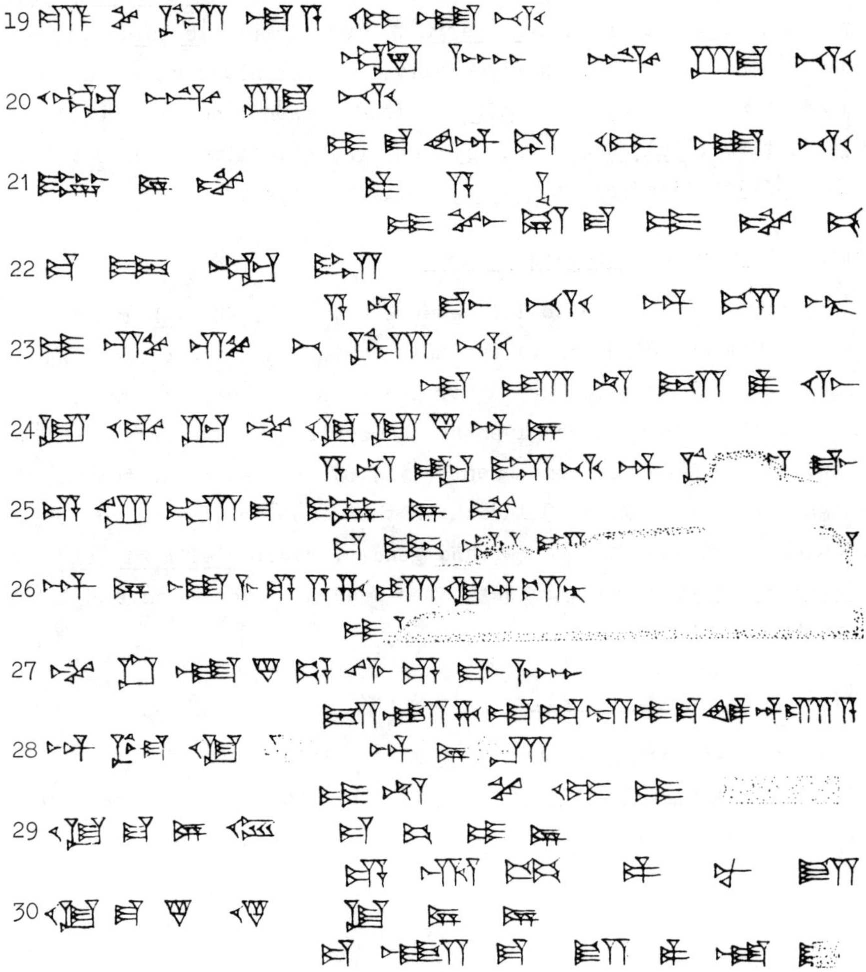

14.1 The preformative of the 1st person singular

In the I/1 conjugation the preformative vowel of the 1st person singular is different from that of the 3rd person, e.g., aprus 'I cut' (cf. ašām 'I purchased' CH 9), iprus 'he cut' (#7.4). However, in the II and III conjugations the preformative vowel of the 1st person singular is the same as that of the 3rd person singular, namely u, e.g., uparris, ušapris. For example, ušellâ (III/1 from elû) "I will raise up here."

14.2 Masculine noun plural in ūtu

Some nouns form their plurals like the adjective (dannu/dannūtu, #9.2) in ūtu rather than ū (šarrū). For example, eṭlūtu 'young men' (line 34). This is especially true for nouns which can be used as adjectives, e.g., mītu 'a dead person' (noun), 'dead' (adjective); balṭu 'a living person' (noun), 'live' (adjective). Thus mītūtu 'dead ones', balṭūtu 'living ones'.

14.3 Logograms to indicate verbs

Logograms can be used to indicate verbs, e.g., KÚ = akālu 'to eat'. The Akkadian equivalent must be put into the correct Akkadian verbal form (cf. #5.6 for nouns in the correct case). Frequently aids will be given by the scribe through determinatives (#6.20), or phonetic complements (#14.8). For example, the MEŠ sign after KÚ in line 19 indicates that the verbal form is plural; context indicates the number and gender, e.g., ušellâ mītūti ikkalū balṭūti "I will raise up the dead here consuming the living."

14.4 The comparative eli

The preposition eli is used to indicate the comparative. For example, eli balṭūti ima''idū mītūti "the dead will be more numerous than the living."

14.5 Speaking formula

In SB the following formula to introduce direct speech is used in full or in part: PN pâšu īpušma iqabbi izzakkara ana PN_2, literally "PN opened his mouth, while speaking, saying to PN_2" = "PN spoke to PN_2 as follows." For example, ātû pâšu īpušma iqabbi izzakkara ana rabīti dIštar "The gatekeeper spoke to Lady Ishtar." Note in this formula the use of the I/2 present of zakāru (izzakkar), sometimes with ventive (izzakkara).

14.6 The "poetic ventive"

A further use of the ventive (other than its dative and lexical uses, #4.12 - #4.13) especially in literary texts is the so-called "poetic ventive" where its precise meaning cannot be ascertained. Examples: izzakkara in the speaking formula (#14.5); ašattâ "I will have to drink" (line 33).

14.7 Circumstantial clauses

In the phrase "the man came weeping" the word 'weeping' indicates the state the man was in while coming or the circumstances of his coming, therefore it is circumstantial. In Akkadian verbs in circumstantial phrases are placed in the present while the preceding verb (in the preterite) will have an enclitic ma. Examples: pâšu īpušma iqabbi izzakkara, literally "opened his mouth, while speaking, saying"; ērumma ātû izzakkara "the gatekeeper entered saying."

14.8 Phonetic complements

A phonetic complement is a sign placed after a logogram indicating that the logogram should have the same ending as the phonetic complement. The phonetic complement is usually one of the signs of the basic sign list. For example, GAL-ti = rabīti, GAL being the logogram for rabû 'great' (141), the ti being the phonetic complement indicating how rabû should be read (feminine singular genitive).

14.9 The irregular verb uzuzzu

The irregular verb uzuzzu 'to stand' has the following I/1 forms: preterite izziz, present izzaz, imperative iziz (feminine izizzī). This verb should not be confused with zâzu 'to divide' or ezēzu 'to be furious'.

14.10 Assimilation of consonants III (see #7.10 & #9.3)

Another of the consonants that assimilate to a following consonant is b, which assimilates to a following m. For example, ērumma (< ērubma) ātû "the gatekeeper entered."

14.11 The demonstrative pronoun annû

The demonstrative pronoun annû is declined as an adjective: annû, annītu, annûtu, annâtu. The feminine form annītu standing alone has a neutral meaning. For example, Ereškigal annīta ina šemîša "When Ereshkigal heard this." The feminine singular form can also be used as an interjection. Examples: annītu mē aḫātki ^{d}Ištar "Behold your sister Ishtar"; annītu mē anāku itti ^{d}Anunnaki mê ašatti "Behold now I will have to drink water with the Anunnaki" (line 32).

14.12 Modification of rule three in Assyrian

In accord with the Assyrian preference of representing a Babylonian i vowel as e, an i followed by an ' (aleph) will go to ē in Assyrian, not ī as in Babylonian (#2.5). Since this text of Ishtar comes from Nineveh it naturally contains many Assyrian elements. For example, ēriqu (not īriqu) in line 29.

Chapter 15

THE DESCENT OF ISHTAR
Lines 31-80

15.0 The Descent of Ishtar lines 31-80

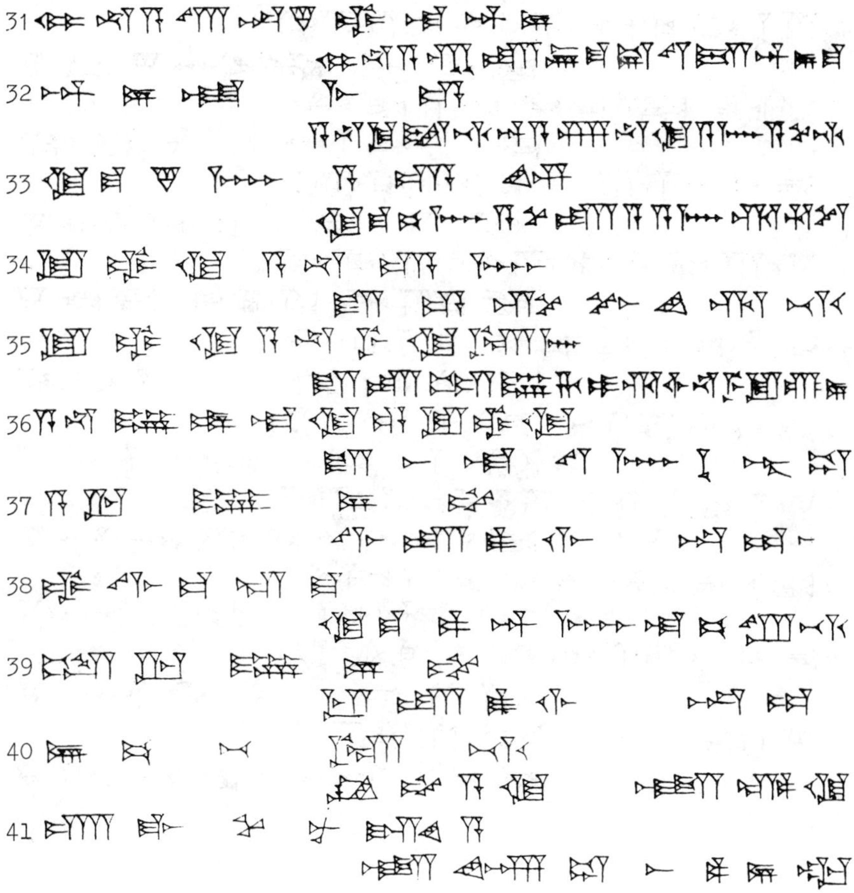

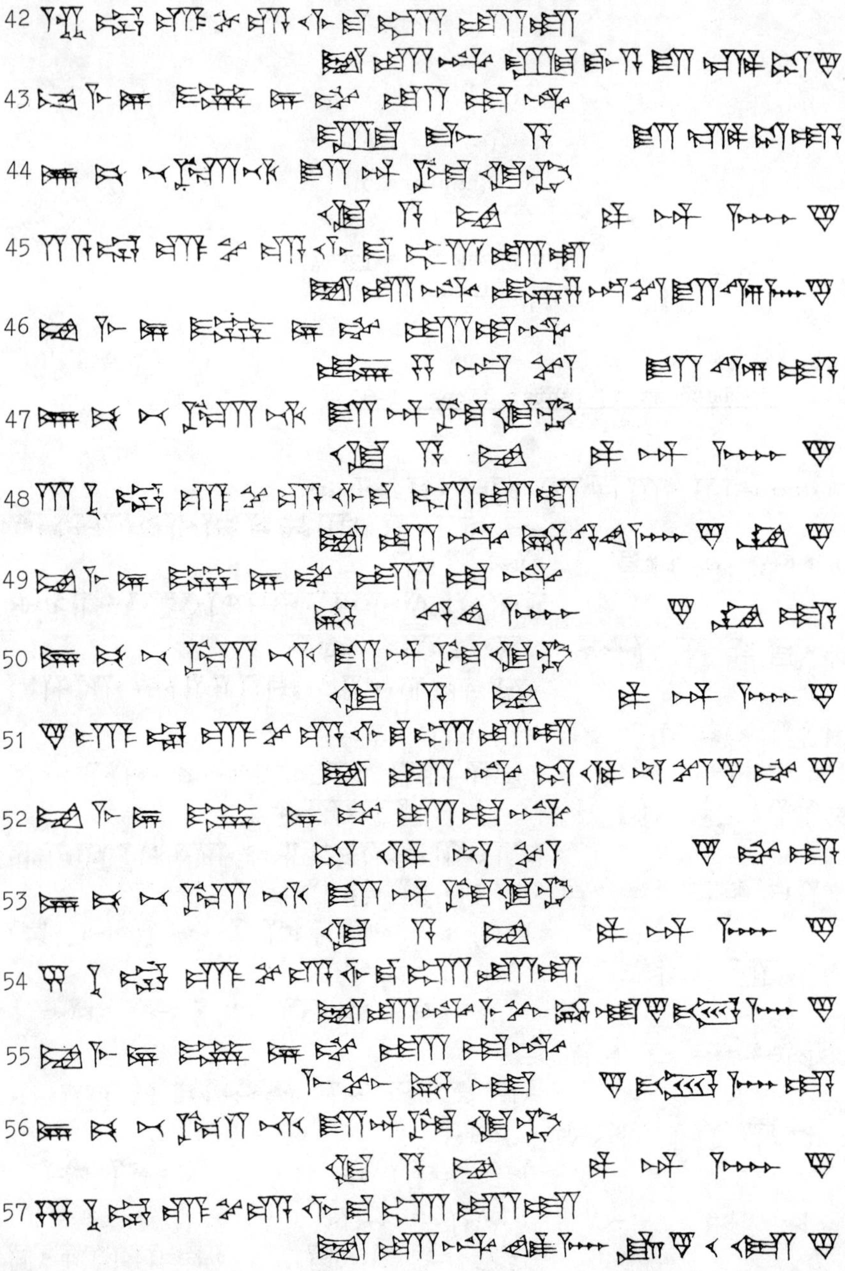

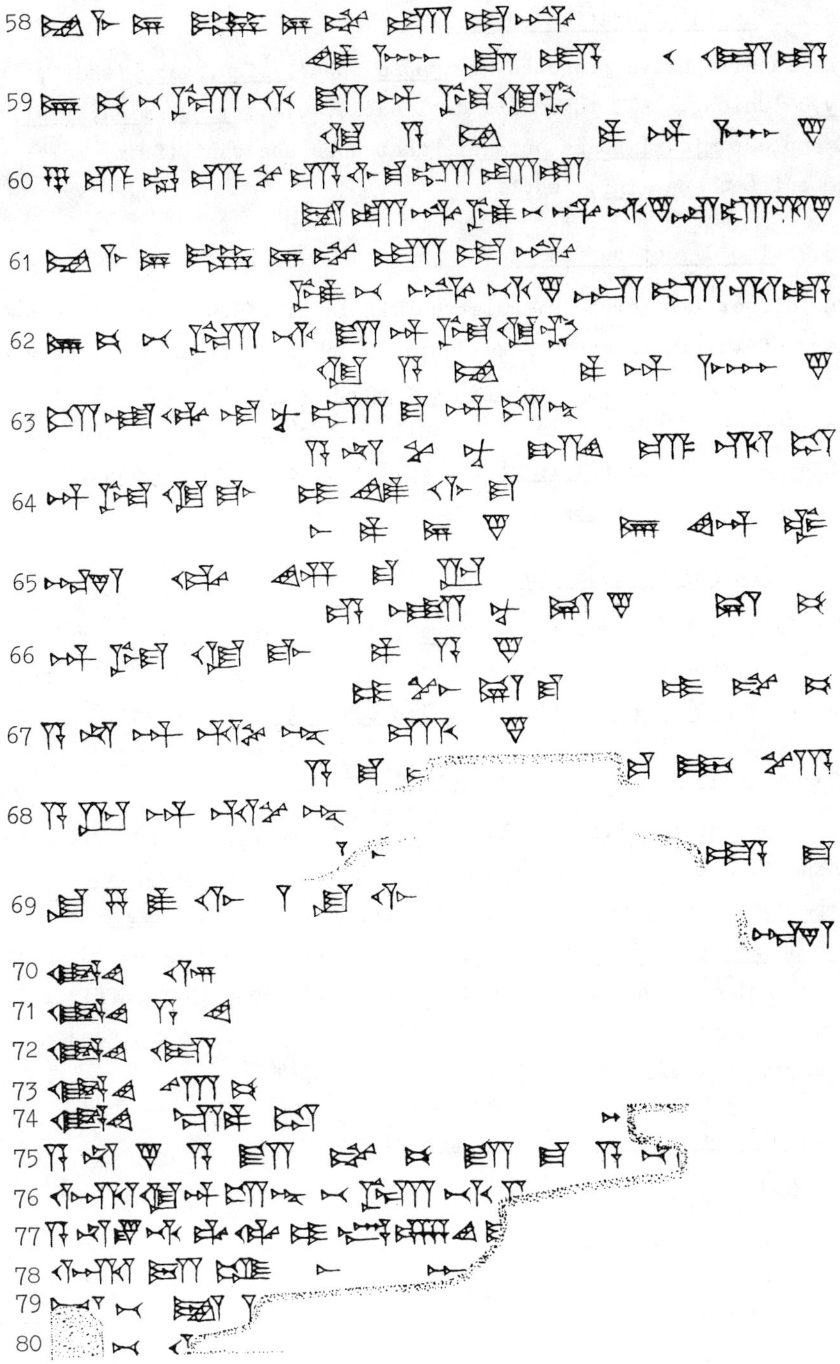

15.1 The interrogative pronouns

The interrogative pronouns are *mannu* 'who', *mīnu*, *minû* 'what', *ayyû* 'which'. All three are declinable, e.g., *minû*, *minâ*, *minî*. Examples: *minâ libbaša ublanni* "what does she want (from) me?"; *ammēni* (< *ana mīni*) 'why'.

15.2 The direct suffix ni

The direct 1st person singular suffix is *ni* (#9.6). On the analogy of the indirect suffixes which often are attached to the ventive form (#9.6, e.g., *petašši* (< *petâm* + *ši*) 'open for her') the direct suffix *ni* also frequently attaches itself to the ventive *am*. Examples: *ublanni* (< *ūbil* + *am* + *ni*), *ušperdanni* (< *ušperdi* + *am* + *ni*).

15.3 The idiom libbu plus ubla

The idiom *libbu* 'heart' plus *ubla* (I/1 from *wabālu* 'to carry' plus ventive) means 'to want', 'to desire', 'to yearn for'. For example, *libbī ubla* 'I wanted', *libbašu ubla* 'he wanted'.

15.4 The idiom kabattu plus neperdû

The idom *kabattu* 'liver' plus *neperdû* 'to be bright' (#13.14) means 'to be happy'. Examples: *ultu libbaša inuḫḫu kabtassa ippereddû* "When she is settled and happy" (line 96); *minâ kabtassāma ušperdannīma*, literally, "What has caused her to make me bright?" = "Why has she made me happy?" Note that suffixes are attached to a by-form of *kabattu*, *kabtatu*, thus *kabtassa* is from *kabtatša*.

15.5 Confusion of idioms in line 31

In line 31 there is a confusion of idioms. The first half of the line *minâ libbaša ublanni* contains the idiom 'to want', 'to desire' (#15.3), e.g., "What does she want (from) me" (taking the direct suffix *anni* (#15.2) with an extended meaning here of 'against' or 'from'. The second half of the line *minâ kabtassāma* ušperdannīma contains the idiom 'to be happy' (#15.4), e.g., "Why has she made me happy."

15.6 The ventive ni(m)

In #4.11 the ventive ending a(m) was discussed. However there are two ventive endings, a(m) and ni(m). The ending a(m) is attached to verbal forms without vocalic affixes, e.g., iprus, iprusa(m); taprus, taprusa(m); aprus, aprusa(m); niprus, niprusa(m). The ending ni(m) is attached to verbal forms with vocalic affixes, e.g., iprusū, iprusūni(m); iprusā, iprusāni(m); parsū, parsūni(m), e.g., šallūni "they are taken as spoil."

15.7 The II/1 & III/1 imperative

The II/1 imperative is purris. For example, uppissīma (< uppiš + ši + ma, #7.10b) kīma parṣī labirūti "treat her in accordance with the ancient rites." The III/1 imperative is šupris. For example, šūṣašši (< šūṣi + am + ši) 'strike her'.

15.8 The ordinal numbers

The masculine forms of the ordinal numbers are: first, maḫrû, pānû, ištēn; second, šanû; third, šalšu; fourth, rebû; fifth, ḫamšu; sixth, šeššu; seventh, sebû; eighth, šamnu; ninth, tišû; tenth, ešru. The ordinal numbers normally precede the substantive. Examples: ištēn bāba 'the first gate', šanâ bāba 'the second gate', šalšu bābu, rebû bābu, ḫamšu bābu, šeššu bābu, sebû bābu. Note that unlike the cardinal numbers there is no polarity (#9.11) with the ordinal numbers.

15.9 ša introducing a casus pendens

The genitive indicator ša (#8.5) can introduce a casus pendens (#6.11). It will thus be followed by a resumptive pronominal suffix. For example, ša bēlet erṣetim kī'am parṣūša, literally, "as for the mistress of the netherworld, such are her rites" = "such are the rites of the mistress of the netherworld."

15.10 The dual

In addition to a singular and plural (#3.6) Akkadian has a dual number. It forms its nominative in ā(n) and its oblique in ī(n). The nunation, like mimation, is characteristic of OB only (#3.7).

		Nominative		Oblique
qātu(m)	'hand'	qātā(n)	'two hands'	qātī(n)
īnu(m)	'eye'	īnā(n)	'two eyes'	īnī(n)

The determinative MIN is placed after nouns to indicate that the preceding word is in the dual. For example, inṣabāte ša GEŠTU. MIN-ya = inṣabāte ša uznīya "the rings of my ears." The MEŠ sign (indicating plural) following MIN in line 45 GEŠTU.MIN.MEŠ is unnecessary.

15.11 The conjunction ištu/ultu

The conjunction ištu/ultu 'since', 'after' takes the subjunctive. For example, ultu libbaša inuḫḫu kabtassa ippereddû "after she has settled down and has become happy." The phrase ištu/ultu ullânumma, literally 'from before' means as a conjunction 'no sooner than', 'scarcely', 'ever since'. Examples: ištu ullânumma dIštar ana erṣet lā târi ūridu "Scarcely had Ishtar gone down to the netherworld"; ultu ullânumma dIštar ana erṣet lā târi ūridu "Ever since Ishtar went down to the netherworld" (line 86).

15.12 The phrase elēnušša ušbi

The phrase elēnušša ušbi in line 65 is problematic. The first word seems to be a combination of the preposition elēnu 'above', the locative um (to be met with later in #17.5), and the pronominal suffix ša, i.e., 'over her'. The second word may be from wašābu 'to sit' (though the expected form is ūšib). Thus "she sat down above her (i.e., in the place of honor due to Ereshkigal)." Other scholars take ušbi from a quadriliteral verb šubê'u 'to rush', 'to dash out', i.e., "she rushed at her."

Chapter 16

THE DESCENT OF ISHTAR
Lines 81-125

16.0 The Descent of Ishtar lines 81-125

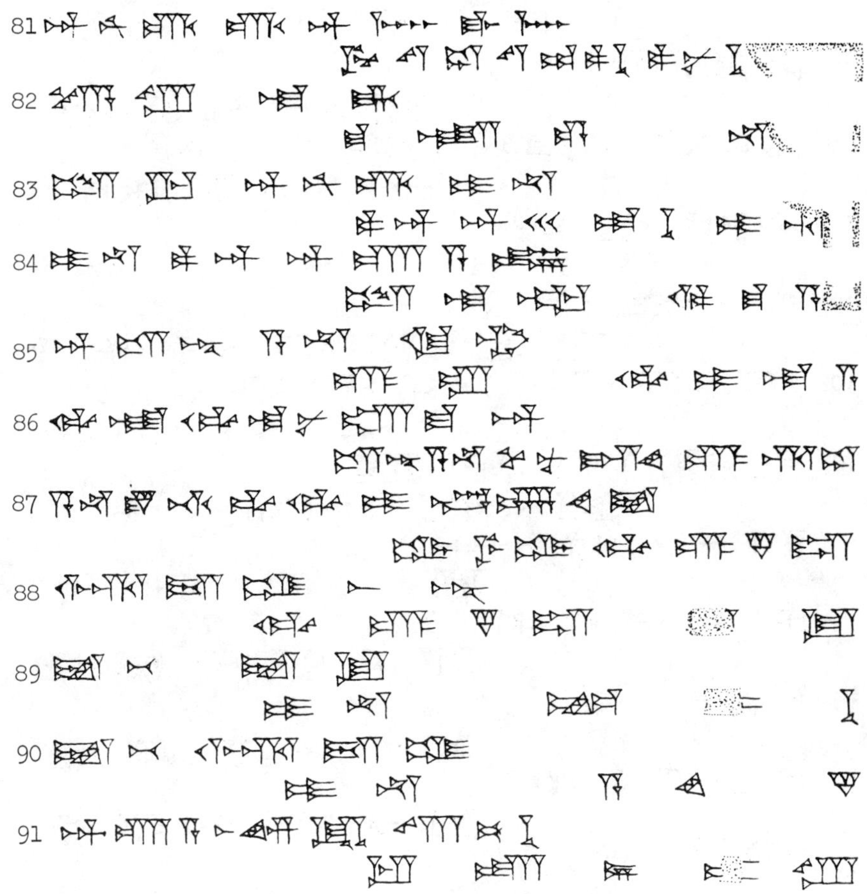

92

93

94

95

96

97

98

99

100

101

102

103

104

105

106

107

108

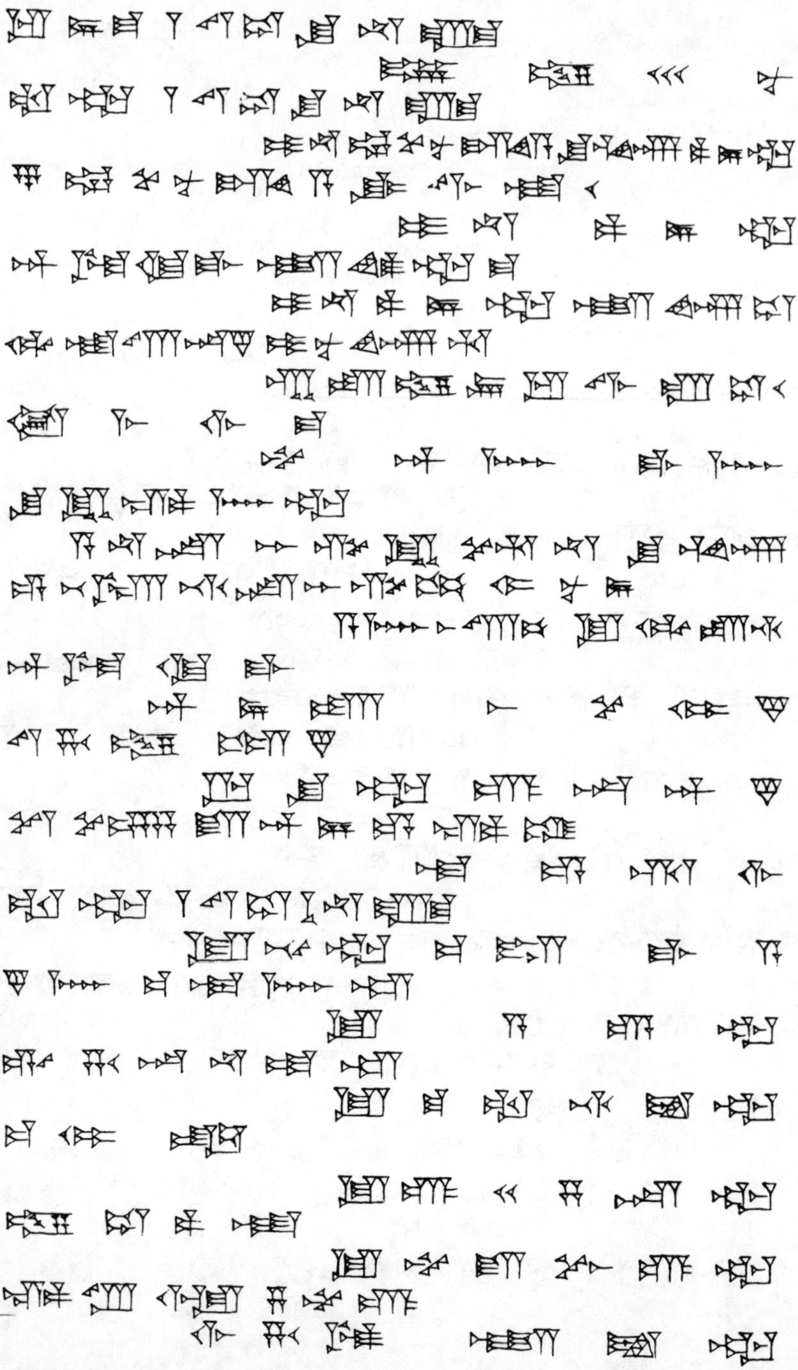

109
110
111
112
113
114
115
116
117
118
119
120
121
122
123
124
125

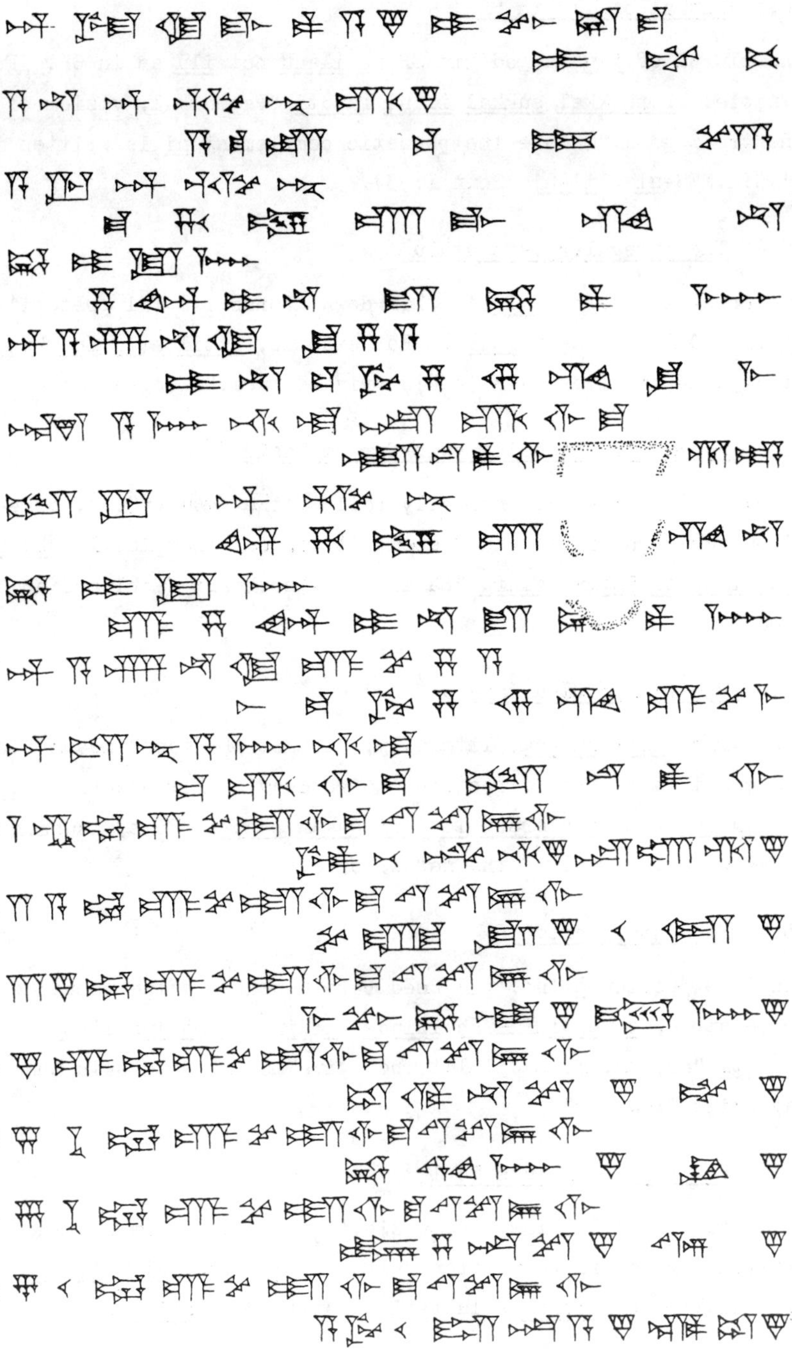

16.1 Plural of ilu in SB

The plural of *ilu* 'a god' in SB is *ilānu* not *ilū* as in OB. For example, ^{d}*Papsukkal sukkal ilāni rabûti* "Papsukkal, vizier of the great gods." Note the phonetic complement *ni* is written in DINGIR.MEŠ-*ni* = *ilāni* (Senn I:63).

16.2 The irregular verb utūlu

The irregular verb *utūlu* 'to lie down' forms its I/1 preterite *ittīl* and its present *ittâl*. For example, *ittīl eṭlu ina kummīšu* "the young man lies down in his private room."

16.3 Adjective preceding noun for emphasis

Although the adjective normally follows the noun (#9.1), sometimes for emphasis it can precede it as, for example, in ^{d}*Ea ina emqi libbīšu ibtani zikru* "Ea in his wise heart fashioned an idea."

16.4 The phrase pānâ šakānu

The phrase *pānâ šakānu*, literally, "to set the face" means "to proceed in a certain direction 'to go away'. For example, *alka* ^{I}*Aṣûšunamir ina bāb erṣet lā târi šukun pānîka* "Come, Asushunamir, go away to the gate of the netherworld."

16.5 The interjection ē

The interjection *ē* 'no!' is used before nouns in the vocative. For example, *ē beltī* ^{mašak}*ḫalziqqu li<di>nūni mê ina libbi lultati* "no, no, my lady! let them give me the waterskin that I may drink from it."

16.6 Shift of sibilants to l

From the end of OB times on, a sibilant appearing before another sibilant or dental very often shifts to *l*, e.g., *št* > *lt*; *šz* > *lz*. Examples: *luštati* > *lultati*; *maštītka* > *maltītka*.

16.7 The 3rd feminine singular taprus

Occasionally in SB the 3rd feminine singular appears as taprus instead of iprus (#11.2). For example, tamḫaṣ pēnša taššuka ubānša "she smote her thigh and bit her finger."

Chapter 17

THE ANNALS OF SENNACHERIB
Column I:1-19

17.0 The Annals of Sennacherib column I:1-19

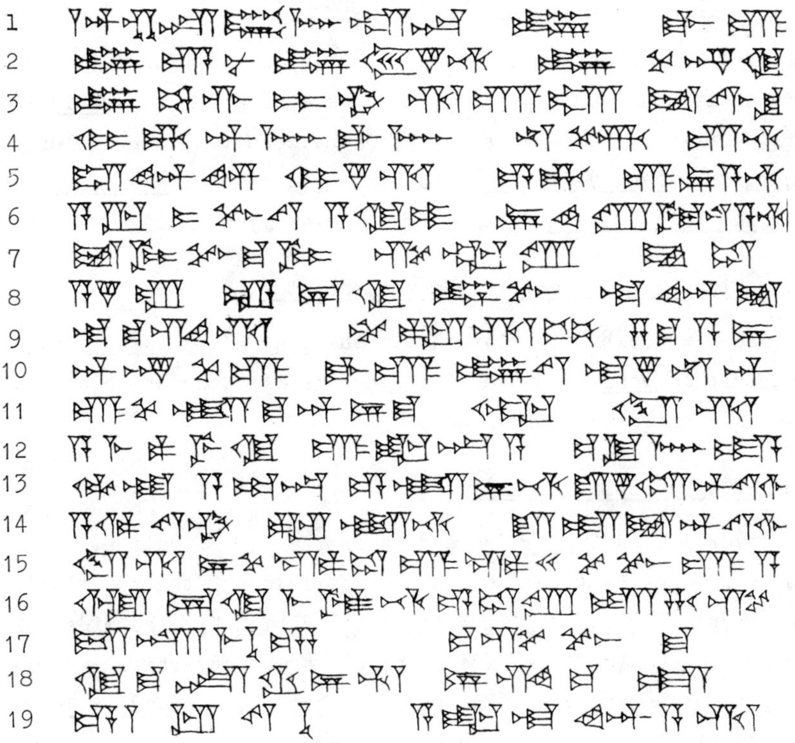

17.1 The ligature EN.ZU

The god Sin in the name Sîn-aḫḫe-erība is written as a backwards ligature, that is, instead of the expected ZU.EN the composite logogram is written EN.ZU. Another example of this phenomenon is the writing of the word *apsû* 'deep water' as ZU.AB instead of the expected AB.ZU.

17.2 The phrase kibrāt erbettim

The phrase *kibrāt erbettim*, literally, 'regions of the four', 'the four regions', denotes 'the entire world'. Although normally the cardinal numbers appear in the *status absolutus* (#8.3A), the feminine form of the number four (*erbu*, *erbittu*) is sometimes construed as a substantive and takes case endings.

17.3 Archaic construct endings in SB

Sometimes in SB nouns, especially participles, which normally form their constructs by dropping case endings (e.g., *pāris* < *pārisu*) preserve archaic endings in the construct. Examples: *sāḫiru* (for *sāḫir*) *damqāti* "who does good deeds"; *mušabriqu* (for *mušabriq*) *zāmâni* "who strikes the enemy with lightning."

17.4 Fixed expressions in status absolutus

Certain fixed expression appear in the *status absolutus* (#8.3E). Examples: *lā šanān* 'unrivaled'; *ṣeḫer rabi*' young and old' (I:50); *zikar u sinniš* 'male and female' (I:51).

17.5 The adverbial ending um

The adverbial ending *um* is used to express the locative. It stands for *ina* (and less often *ana*) followed by the genitive. For example, *qerbum Bābili* = *ina qereb Bābili* "in the midst of Babylon." When suffixes are attached to the adverbial *um* the final *m* is assimilated. Examples: *qerbuššu* < *qerbumšu* = *ina qerbīšu* 'in its midst'; *šēpū'a* < *šēpum-ya* = *ana šēpīya* 'at my feet'.

17.6 Shortened forms of the 3rd person suffixes

In SB the 3rd person pronominal suffixes (#7.13) are often shortened. Examples: dadmêšun 'their homes', napištuš 'his life' (I:24); but note limētīšunu 'their environs' (I:38), bīt niṣirtīšu 'his treasure house' (I:29).

17.7 The adverbial ending iš

The adverbial ending iš has a number of usages two of which are: (1) changing adjectives into adverbs, e.g., damqu 'good', damqiš 'well'; lemnu 'bad', lemniš 'badly'; ēdu 'single', ēdiš 'alone'; (2) replacing the preposition kīma in its meaning of 'as', 'like', e.g., šallatiš = kīma šallati 'as spoil' (I:35).

Chapter 18

THE ANNALS OF SENNACHERIB
Column I:20-42

18.0 The Annals of Sennacherib column I:20-42

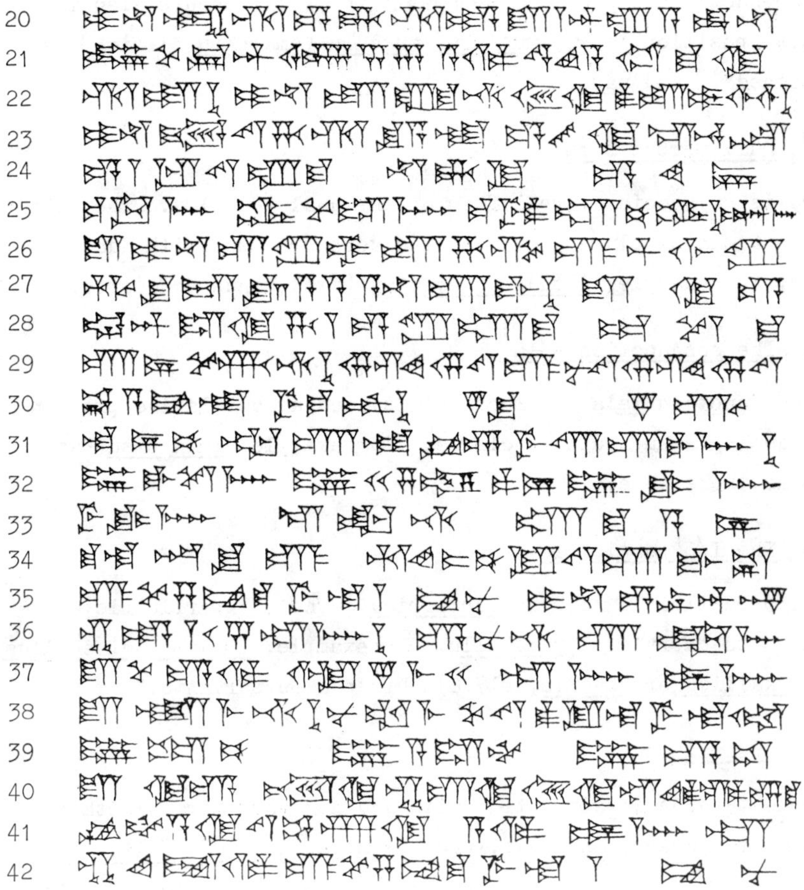

18.1 The I/2 infinitive

The I/2 infinitive form is pitrusu. The I/2 of qerēbu 'to draw near' is qitrubu. For example, ina qitrub tāḫāzi "in the battle onlaught."

18.2 Shift of w to m

From MB on an intervocalic w (a w between vowels) will shift to m. Examples: awīlum > amīlu; lawû > lamû, e.g., alme "I besieged"; ewû > emû, e.g., ušēmi "I turned into" (I:80). With wu''uru 'to send a person or message', wuššuru 'to release', 'to abandon', and wâṣu 'to be small' the shift occurs also in initial position, e.g., mu''uru, muššuru (umaššiiru "[which] he abandoned"), and mâṣu.

18.3 Dual verbal form

There is no special verbal form of the dual (#15.10). The third person feminine plural forms of the verb are used with dual subjects, for example, ikšudā qatāyā "my (two) hands conquered."

18.4 The conjunction mala

The conjunction mala 'as much as' is used as a relative pronoun introducing a subordinate clause. For example, mala bašû "as much as there were."

18.5 The I/3 participle

The I/3 participle form is muptarrisu. The I/3 participle of wabālu 'to carry' is muttabbilu. For example, muttabbilūt ēkalluš (for ēkallišu or ēkalliš, #17.6) "his palace servants."

18.6 Apposition

A word standing in apposition with another word agrees with it in number, gender, and case. For example, ina emūq ^{d}Aššur bēlīya "through the power of Ashur, my lord." When a construct-genitive phrase stands in apposition to a plural it is placed in the singular, for example, *mārē āli bēl ḫiṭṭi* "the rebel citizens."

18.7 Usage of the number signs

The signs for the numbers were given in #6.18. Their use is as follows: Below a hundred the numbers are simply added according to their value, e.g.,  60, 10, 5 = 75; 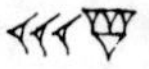 30, 4 = 34 (II:17). After a hundred, values less than ten which appear before the hundred sign serve as multipliers, e.g., 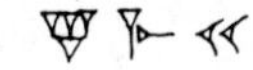 4, 100, 20 = 420; 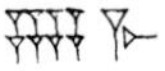 8, 100 = 800 (III:42) After a thousand values of less than a thousand which appear before the thousand sign serve as multipliers, e.g.,  2, 100, 8, 1000 = 208,000 (I:50); 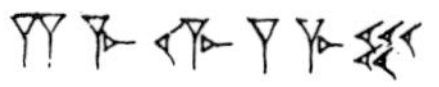 2, 100, 1000, 1, 100, 50 = 200,150 (III:24).

18.8 Plurals of some construct-genitive phrases

Some construct-genitive phrases become so standardized that they are treated as one word, and make their plurals by having plural endings attached to the genitive part only, for example, *bīt dūrāni* 'fortresses' (not *bītāt dūrāni*).

18.9 Phonetic complements II

As stated in #14.8 the phonetic complement is a sign placed after a logogram indicating that the logogram should have the same ending as the phonetic complement. Phonetic complements can also be used with verbal forms, the logogram representing the verb while the phonetic complement indicates how it should be read. For example, the logogram  KUR in  KUR-*ud* has three Akkadian values listed in the third column of the sign list (#14.8) *mātu*, *šadû*, and *kašādu*. The phonetic complement *ud* indicates a choice of *kašādu* since no form of *mātu* or *šadû* could end in *ud*. However, the I/1 preterite of *kašādu* does end in *ud*, *ikšud*. Context indicates that a first person singular is required (since it is in a series with *alme* and *ašlula*) so the form should be read *akšud* "I conquered."

18.10 Gentilic endings

The gentilic or ethnic endings in Akkadian are <u>û</u> and <u>āyu</u>/<u>āya</u>. Examples: <u>Aramû</u> 'Aramaeans', <u>Ṣidunnāya</u> 'Sidonian' (II:51).

Chapter 19

THE ANNALS OF SENNACHERIB
Column I:43-82

19.0 <u>The Annals of Sennacherib column I:43-82</u>

43
44
45
46
47
48
49
50
51
52
53
54
55
56
57
58
59
60
61
62
63
64

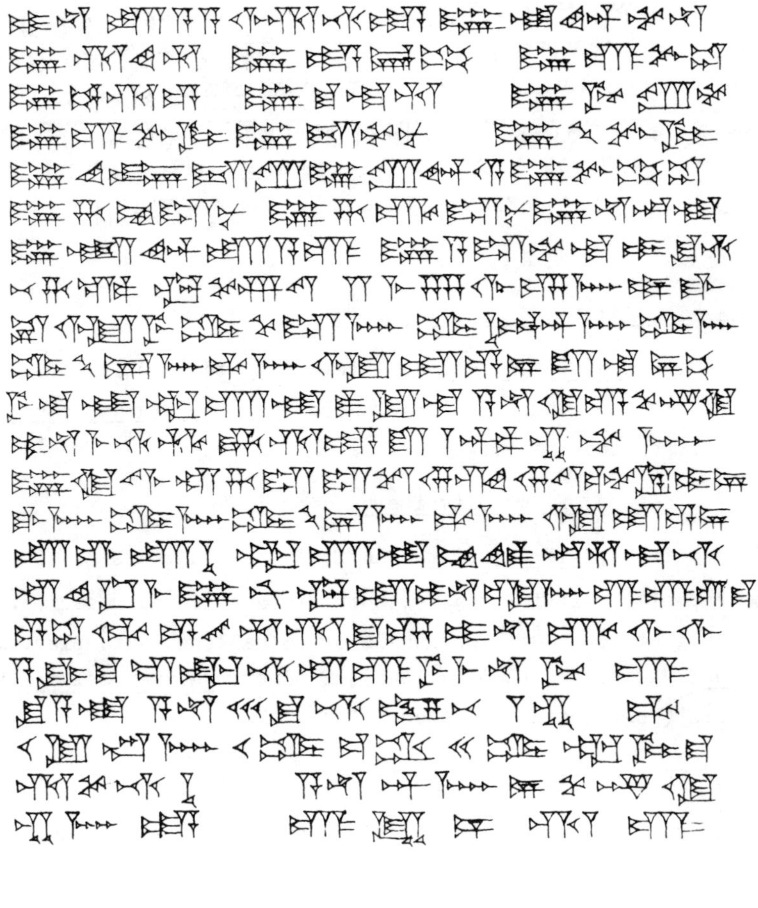

19.1 The idiom ana eššūti ṣabātu

The idiom <u>ana</u> <u>eššūti</u> <u>ṣabātu</u>, literally, "to take over for newness" means 'to reorganize'. For example, <u>nagû</u> <u>šu'ātu</u> <u>ana</u> <u>eššūti</u> <u>aṣbat</u> "I reorganized that region."

19.2 Measure of capacity imēru

Mainly in NA, <u>imēru</u> (written ANŠE) 'homer' appears as a measure of capacity. It is used for both dry and liquid measures, and is equivalent to about 2.8 bushels or 25 gallons. Examples: 10 <u>imēr</u> <u>karāni</u> "10 homers (300 gallons) of wine"; <u>20</u> <u>imēr</u> <u>suluppī</u> "20 homers (56 bushels) of dates."

19.3 The adverbial ending išam

The adverbial ending <u>išam</u> consists of the adverbial ending <u>iš</u>

(#17.7) and the accusative ending am. It is used to form adverbs of time, e.g., warḫišam 'monthly', ūmišam 'daily', dārišam 'for ever'.

19.4 The I/2 stative

The I/2 stative form is pitrus. The third person masculine plural form is pitrusū. The I/2 3rd masculine plural stative of kanāšu 'to submit' is kitnušū, for example, ša ultu ullâ ana šarrāni abbīya lā kitnušū "(The Kassites) who since time immemorial had not become the subjects of my royal ancestors."

19.5 The asseverative lū

The particle lū has previously been met as a coordinating conjunction (#8.1) and as a precative (#9.5). Another usage of this particle is to serve as an asseverative---to emphasize the verbal form. It can thus be translated as 'surely', 'indeed', or 'certainly'. Note that the asseverative lū (unlike the precative lū) is normally not joined to the following verbal form. Thus lū aprus is 'I surely cut', but the precative is luprus 'let me cut'. For example, lū allik "I surely marched."

19.6 The superlative

The superlative is expressed in Akkadian in two ways: (1) by use of construct-genitive constructions with (a) the adjective and noun, e.g., rabât ^{d}Igigi "greatest among the Igigi gods", or (b) the singular and plural of the same noun, e.g., bēlet bēlēti 'foremost lady', ilat ilāti 'supreme goddess'; (2) by use of the III/1 stative and infinitive forms, e.g., ašru šupšuqu "a most difficult area"; ašar ina kussî šupšuqu "where it was too narrow for my sedan chair" (IV:5).

19.7 The adverbial ending āniš

The adverbial ending āniš is a variant of the more regular adverbial <u>iš</u> ending (#17.7) with the same meanings, for example, <u>rímāniš</u> "like a wild bull."

Chapter 20

THE ANNALS OF SENNACHERIB
Column II:1-36

20.0 <u>The Annals of Sennacherib column II:1-36</u>

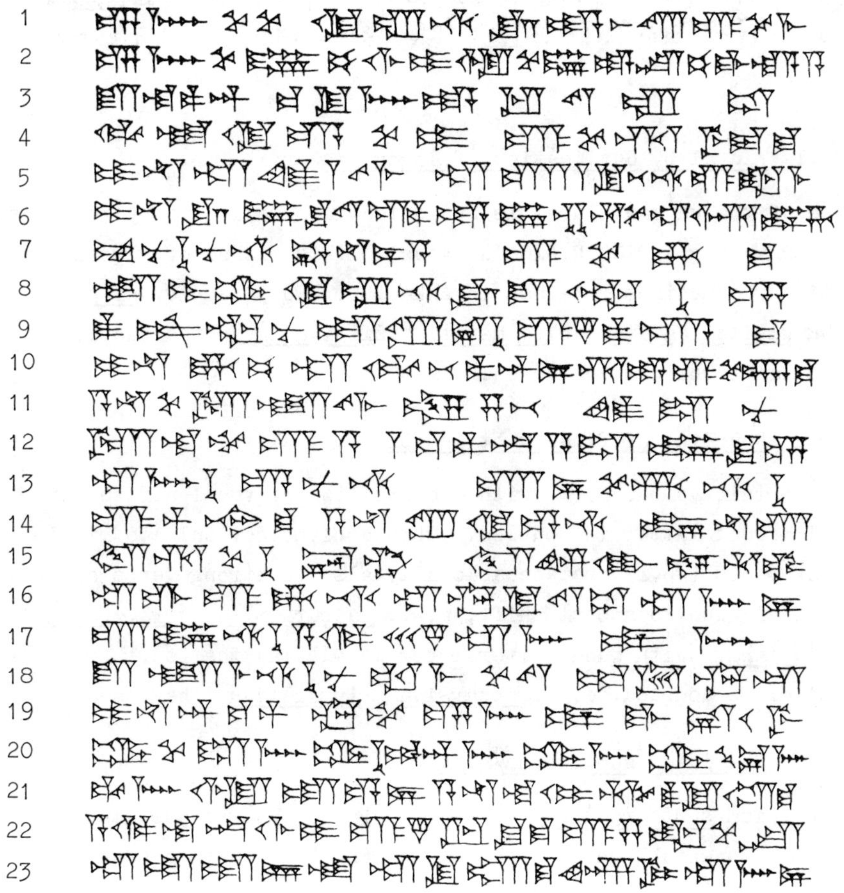

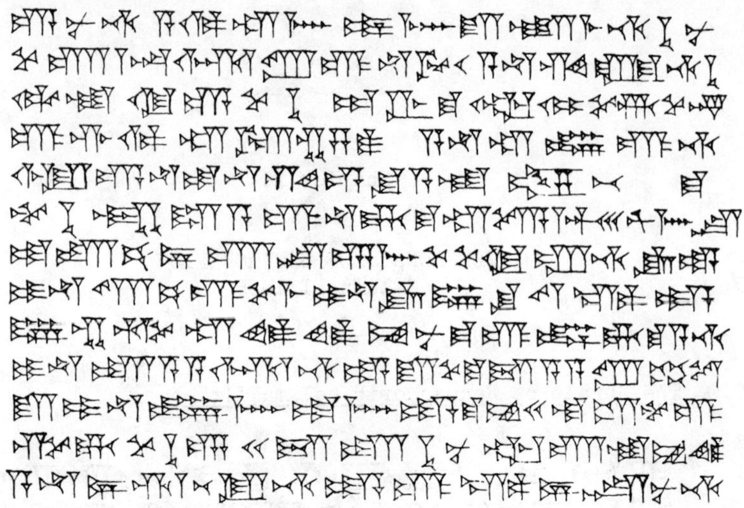

20.1 Plural by duplication of logograms

One of the ways a plural is indicated in Sumerian is by repeating the word e.g., DINGIR.DINGIR 'gods'. This method of plural formation is sometimes retained in Akkadian. For example, niše KUR.KUR kišitti qātīya = nišē mātāti kišitti qātīya "the people of the lands which I conquered."

20.2 Doubling of final root letter

In certain verbal forms with the addition of vocal affixes the third root letter is doubled. This applies not only to middle weak verbs (#6.15) but occasionally also to strong verbs as well, possibly due to accent shift, e.g., tašpura > tašpurra, iddina > iddinna. With quadriliteral verbs (#13.12) the fourth root letter is doubled, e.g., ipparšidū > ipparšiddū 'they escaped'.

20.3 The idiom šubta ramû/nadû

The idiom šubta ramû/nadû, literally, "to throw a dwelling" means "to establish or erect a dwelling," "to settle oneself."

Often the verb is used elliptically with *šubtu* omitted, for example, *ina* ^{āl}*Ḫardišpi* ^{āl}*Bit-*^{I}*Kubatti* *ušarme* "I settled (them) in Hardishpi and Bit-Kubatti."

20.4 The plural form of the genitive indicator

The old plural form of the genitive indicator *ša* (#8.5) is retained in some nominal constructions, e.g., *šūt* *rēši*, literally, "those of the head" = 'commanders', 'generals'.

20.5 The IV/1 of initial aleph verbs

In the IV/1 conjugation of initial *aleph* verbs the *aleph* dissimilates back to the *n*, e.g., *amāru* 'to see', *in'amir* > *innammir* 'he was seen'; *abātu* II 'to flee', *in'abit* > *innabit* 'he fled'. In some initial aleph verbs the reverse process takes place, the *n* assimilating to the *aleph*, e.g., *adāru* 'to worry', *in'adir* > *i''adir* 'he was worried'; *abātu* 'to destroy', *in'abit* > *i''abit* 'it was destroyed'.

20.6 The accusative of condition or state

The accusative used by itself often has adverbial meaning, cf., for example, the accusative of specification (#10.2). A further use of this adverbial accusative is to designate a condition or state. Examples: *emūqa* 'by force', *ḫamṭa* 'immediately', *lā mīna*(*m*) 'without number'.

20.7 The idiom adi lā bašî alāku

The idiom *adi* *lā* *bašî* *alāku*, literally, "to go to non-existence" means "to come to naught." The III/1 means "to bring to naught," for example, *adi* *lā* *bašî* *ušālikšu* "I brought him to naught."

20.8 Quantitative pronouns

The quantitative pronouns indicating 'all', e.g., *kalû*, *siḫirtu*, *gimru*, *gimirtu* etc., can either stand in the construct before the words they qualify (e.g., *ašared kal malkī* "foremost of all princes", *eli gimri āšib parakki* "over every king", *siḫirti ummâni* "all of the artisans") or they can stand in apposition after these words. In the latter case they must have a resumptive pronominal suffix, e.g., *nagû ana gimirtīšu* "the entire district", *šarrāni* ^{māt}*Amurri kalîšun* "all the kings of Amurru" (II:58).

20.9 Indefinite pronouns

The indefinite pronouns are formed from the interrogative pronouns *mannu* 'who', *minû*, *mīnu* 'what, *ayyû* 'which' (#15.1). From *mannu* comes the forms *manman*, *mamman*, *mamma*, *manāma*, *manamma* 'whoever', 'anyone at all'. With negatives the translation is 'no one', e.g., *mamman lā išmû* "no one heard." From *mīnu* comes the form *mimma* 'whatever', 'anything at all', e.g., *mimma šumšu* 'whatever its name' = 'everything whatsoever', #8.2. From *ayyû* comes the form *ayyumma* 'whichever', 'whatever'.

Chapter 21

THE ANNALS OF SENNACHERIB
Column II:37-III:49

21.0 The Annals of Sennacherib column II:37-III:49

Column II:37-83

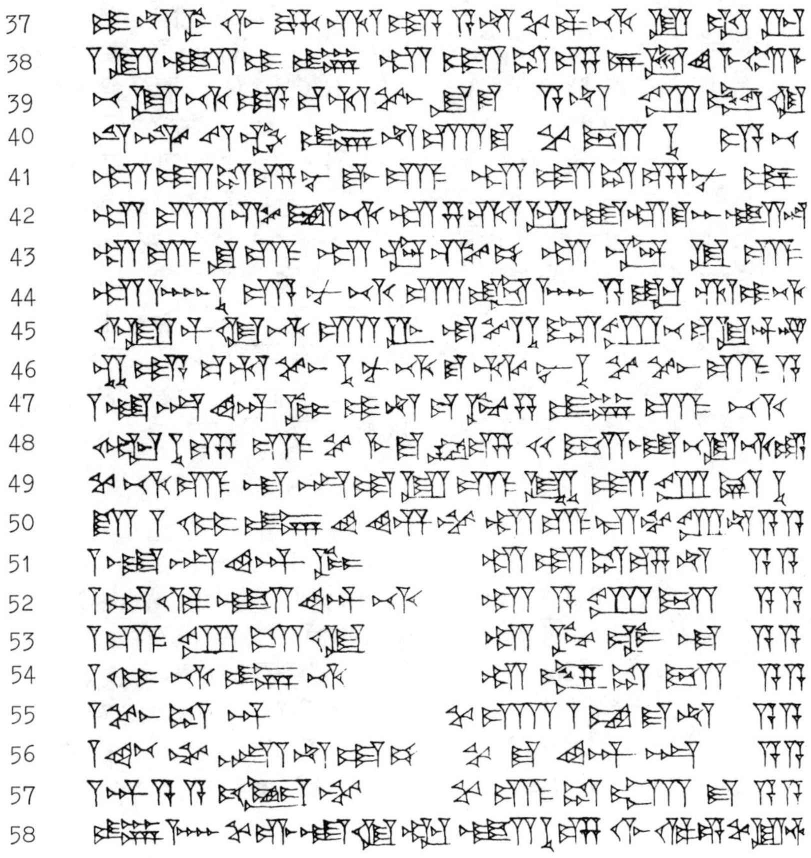

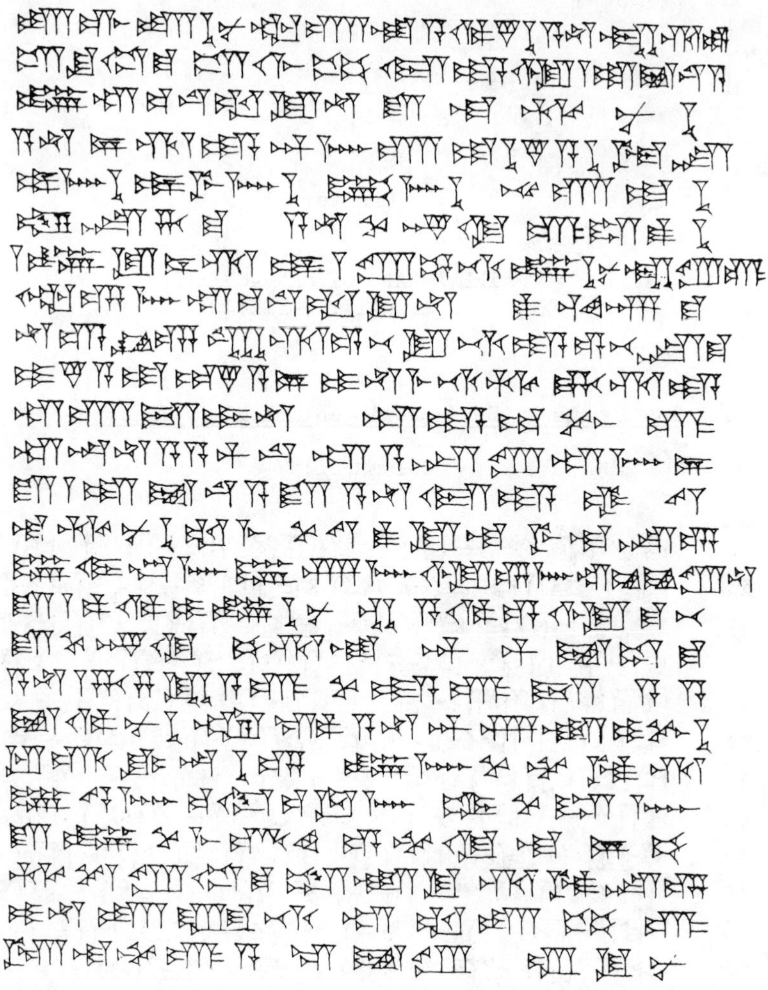

Column III:1-49

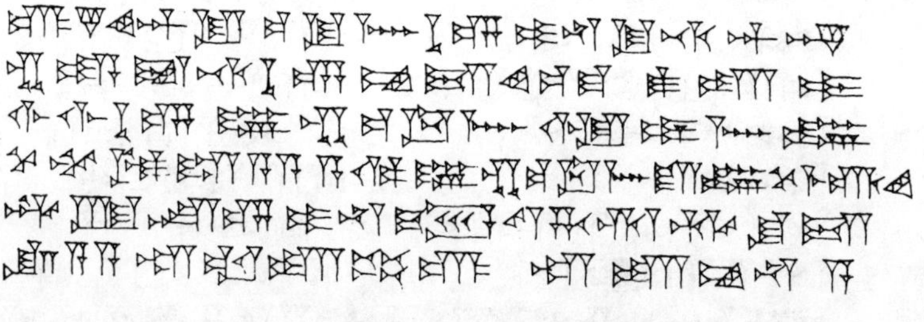

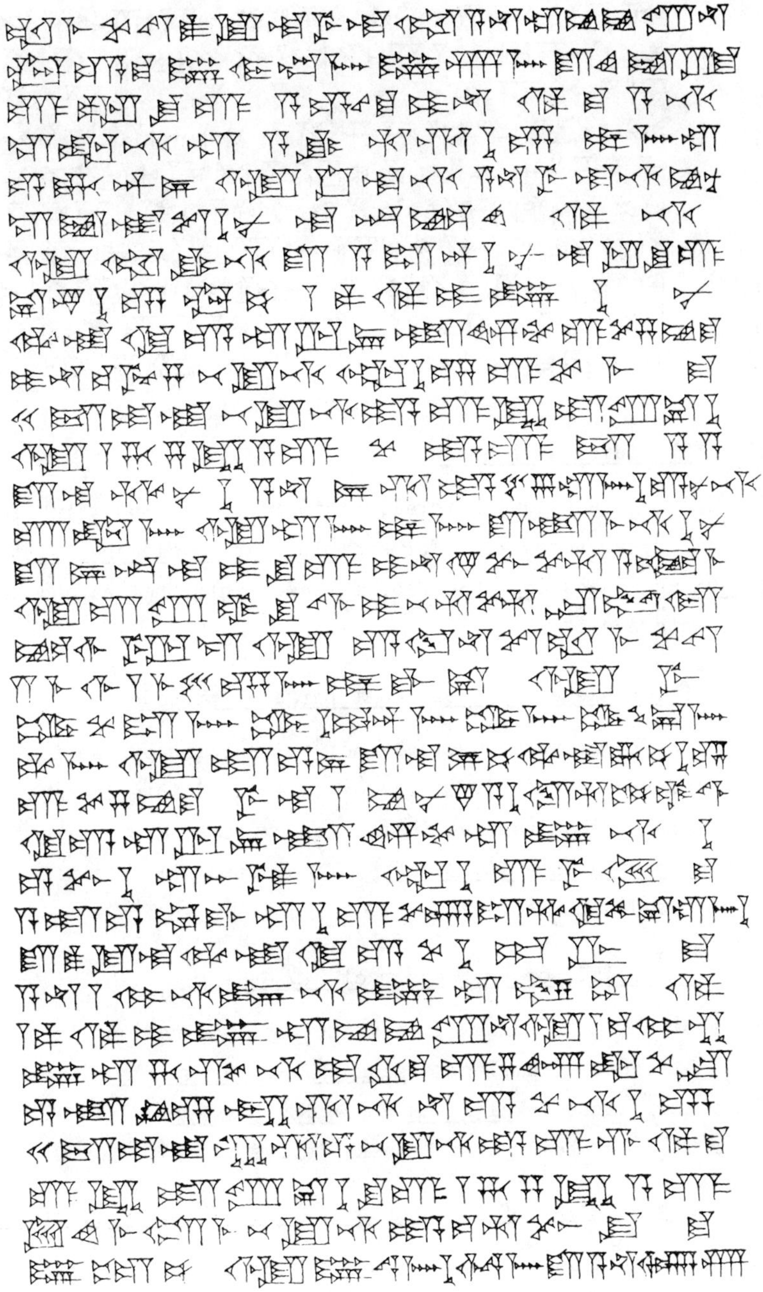

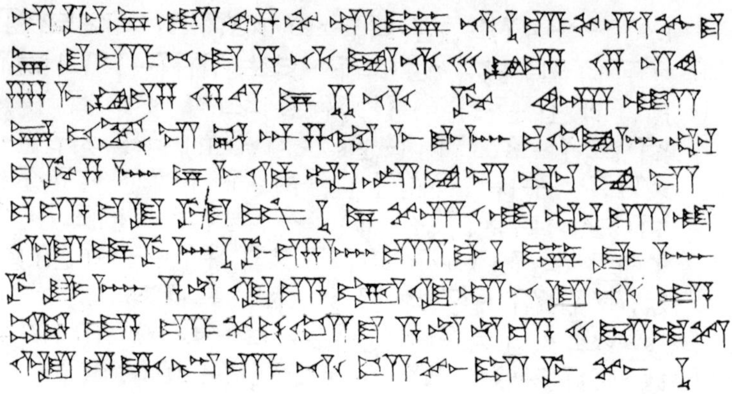

21.1 The idiom šadâ emēdu

The idiom *šadâ emēdu*, literally, "to reach the mountain" means "to disappear forever." For example, *ana ruqqi qabal tâmtim innabitma šadâšu ēmid* "He fled far away into the sea and disappeared forever."

21.2 Interchange of independent personal pronouns

In SB the genitive/accusative and dative forms of the independent personal pronouns (#13.7) are sometimes used interchangeably. For example, *šâšu* (dative instead of expected accusative *šâtu*) *aššassu mārēšu mārātīšu...assuḫ* "I deported him, his wife, his sons, his daughters...."

21.3 Adverbial force of abstract ūtu ending

The abstract *ūtu* ending (#4.3) with a pronominal suffix has adverbial force. Examples: *rēṣussun* (< *rēṣūtu* + *šun*) means 'to their assistance'; *balṭussun* (< *balṭūtu* + *šun*), literally, "in their state of being alive" means 'alive'.

21.4 Assimilation of consonants IV (cf. #7.10, #9.3, #14.10)

A. In NA an infixed *t* in verbs with initial *m* will shift to *d*, that is, there is regressive assimilation of unvoiced *t* to voiced *m*. For example, the I/2 of *mahāṣu* 'to strike' is *imdaḫiṣ* < *imtaḫiṣ*, e.g., *amdaḫiṣ* 'I fought'.

B. In NA an *r* frequently assimilates to the following consonant, e.g., *arnabu* > *annabu* 'hare', *qarnu* > *qannu* 'horn', *arnu* > *annu* 'crime'.

SIGN LIST

The signs in column I are arranged according to their pertinent characteristics, e.g., horizontal wedges  ,  ,  , signs containing the elements  ,  ,  , then vertical wedges  ,  . Column II contains the basic sign values (vowel, consonant plus vowel, vowel plus consonant); column III the simple logograms; column IV the composite logograms. Composite logograms whose first sign consists of a determinative can be found under the second sign in the group. Only signs which occur in the texts of this Manual are listed here. For more detailed sign lists, see those listed in the Suggestions for Further Reading on page 179.

	I	II	III	IV
	SIGN	SYLLABIC VALUE	SIMPLE LOGOGRAM	COMPOSITE LOGOGRAM
1		aš	= <u>ina</u> 'in'	
2		ḫal		 URU.ḪAL.ṢU = <u>^{āl}ḫalṣu</u> 'fortification'
3		muq		
4		ba		
5		zu sú ṣú		

	I	II	III	IV
6		su	KUŠ = <u>mašku</u> 'skin' = determinative before items made of skin SU = <u>râbu</u> 'substitute'	
7	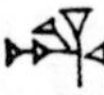	bal		
8		ád		
9		t/ṭar	SILA = <u>sūqu</u> 'street'	
10	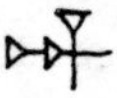	an	DINGIR = <u>ilu</u> 'god' = determinative before gods	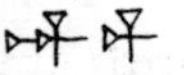 AN.BAR = <u>parzillu</u> 'iron'  NA$_4$.AN.GUG.ME = <u>^{aban}sāndu</u> 'red sandstone'
11				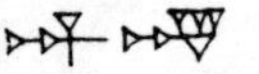 DINGIR.AŠŠUR = <u>$^{d}\mathrm{Aššur}$</u> 'Ashur'  KUR.AŠŠUR.KI = <u>$^{\mathrm{māt}}\mathrm{Aššur}$</u> 'Assyria'
12	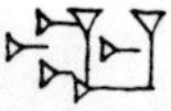	ka	ZÚ = <u>šinnu</u> 'ivory'	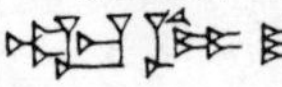 ZÚ.LUM.MA = <u>suluppu</u> 'date'
13		nak		
14	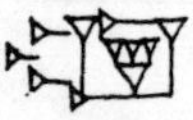		KÚ = <u>akālu</u> 'to eat'	
15		eri	URU = <u>ālu</u> 'city' = determinative before cities	
16	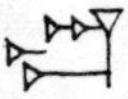		ÌR = <u>wardu</u> 'slave'	
17	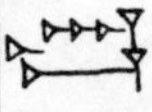		ITU = <u>warḫu</u> 'month'	
18	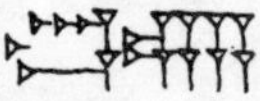	šaḫ	ŠAḪ = <u>šaḫû</u> 'pig'	

	I	II	III	IV
19	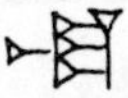	la		
20	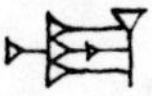			 GIŠ.APIN = $^{\underline{iṣ}}$<u>epinnu</u> 'plow'
21		maḫ		
22	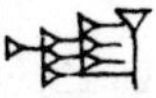	tu		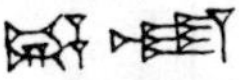 NA_4.TU = $^{\underline{aban}}$<u>yaraḫḫu</u> 'ruby'?
23	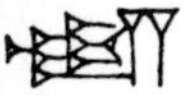	le/i		
24		pap	PAP = <u>aḫu</u> 'brother'	 LÚ.KÚR = $^{\underline{amēl}}$<u>nakru</u> 'enemy'
25		mu	MU = <u>nīšu</u> 'life' = <u>šumu</u> 'name' = <u>zikru</u> 'name'	
26		qa		
27		kàd/t		
28		ru šub/p		
29		be bat/ṭ mid/t til ziz		
30		na		 NA_4.RÚ.A = $^{\underline{aban}}$<u>narû</u> 'stela'
31		šir		
32		kul zir	NUMUN = <u>zēru</u> 'seed'	
33	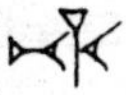	ti		 TI.LA = <u>balāṭu</u> 'life'
34		bar maš		 MAŠDÁ = <u>muškênu</u> 'common citizen'
35		nu	NU = <u>lā</u> 'not'	 KUR.NU.GI_4.(A) = <u>erṣet</u> <u>lā</u> <u>târi</u> 'the netherworld'
36		kun		

	I	II	III	IV
37	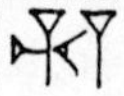	ḫu pag	MUŠEN = <u>eṣṣūru</u> 'bird' = determinative after birds	
38		nam		
39		ig/k/q		 GIŠ.IG = $^{\underline{is}}$<u>daltu</u> 'door'
40		mut		
41		rad/t		
42		ṣí/zi		
43		ge/i		
44		re/i d/tal		
45	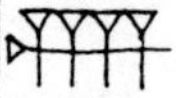	nun zil	NUN = <u>rubû</u> 'prince'	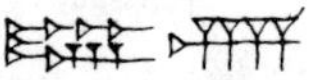 LÚ.NUN = $^{\underline{amēl}}$<u>rubû</u> 'prince'
46		kab		
47		tim		
48	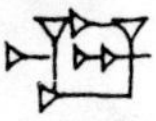	ag/k/q		
49		en	EN = <u>bēlu</u> 'lord'	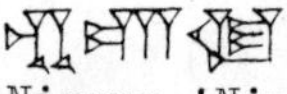 EN.LÍL.KI = <u>Nippur</u> 'Nippur' 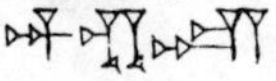 DINGIR.EN.ZU = ^{d}<u>Sîn</u> 'Sin'  ^{I}DINGIR.EN.ZU.ŠEŠ.MEŠ-<u>eri</u>-<u>ba</u> = ^{I}<u>Sîn</u>-<u>aḫḫē</u>-<u>erîba</u> 'Sennacherib' 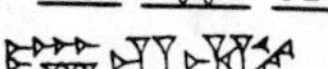 LÚ.EN.NAM = $^{\underline{amēl}}$<u>bēl</u> <u>piḫāti</u> 'commissioner'
50	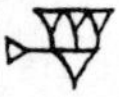	šur		
51				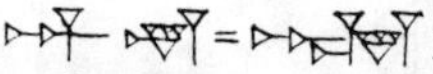 DINGIR.INANNA = ^{d}<u>Ištar</u> 'Ishtar'
52		sa		
53		kár		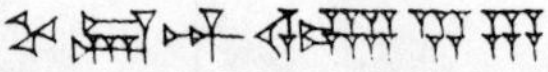 KUR.KÁR.DINGIR-<u>dun</u>-<u>yá</u>-<u>àš</u> = $^{\underline{māt}}$<u>Kār</u>-^{d}<u>Dunyaš</u> 'Babylon'

	I	II	III	IV
54			GÚ = kišādu 'neck'	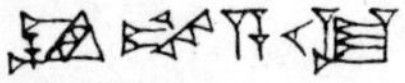 GÚ.DU$_8$.A.KI = Kutâ 'Cutha'
55			GUN = biltu 'tribute'	
56	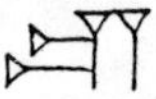	g/qur		
57	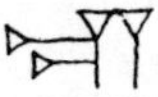	se/i		
58		reš riš sag šak	SAG = rēšu 'head'	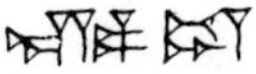 SAG.DU = qaqqadu 'head'  GIŠ.SAG.KUL = ^{iṣ}sikkūru 'lock'
59				 GIŠ.MÁ = ^{iṣ}elippu 'boat'
60		ṭir		
61	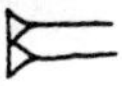	tab/p		
62			4 = erbu, erbettu 'four'	
63	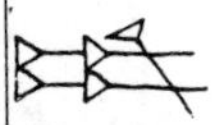	šum tag/k		
64	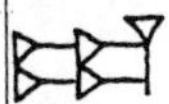	ab/p		
65		ug/k/q		
66		as/ṣ/z		
67	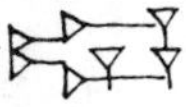		KÁ = bābu 'gate'	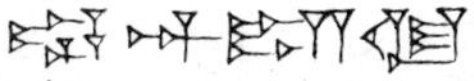 KÁ.DINGIR.RA.KI = Bābilu 'Babylon'  KÁ.GAL = abullu 'city gate'
68				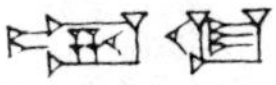 NINA.KI = Ninūa 'Nineveh'
69	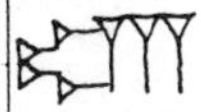	um		
70		ta	TA = ultu, ištu 'from'	
71	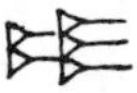	i		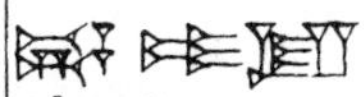 NA$_4$.I.DIB = ^{aban}askuppatu 'threshold'
72		ya/e/i/u		

	I	II	III	IV
73	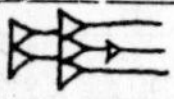	g/kan		
74	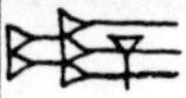		DUMU = *māru* 'son' TUR = *ṣeḫru* 'small'	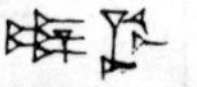 DUMU.MÍ = *martu* 'daughter'  LÚ.BÀNDA = ^{amēl}*šerru* 'child'
75	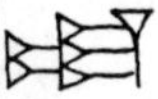	ad/t/ṭ	AD = *abu* 'father'	
76		ṣe/i		
77	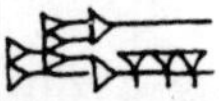	in		
78	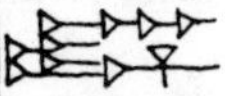	rap		
79		šàr	LUGAL = *šarru* 'king'	
80		ḫir		
81			BÀD = *dūru* 'wall'	
82			SUM = *nadānu* 'to give'	
83		gab/p qab káp	GABA = *irtu* 'breast'	
84			EDIN = *ṣēru* 'field'	
85	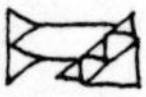	am		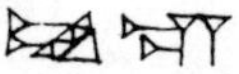 AM.SI = *pīru* 'elephant'
86		ne b/pil kúm		
87		ram		
88		zik		
89				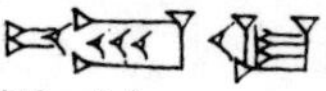 UNU.KI = *Uruk* 'Uruk'
90	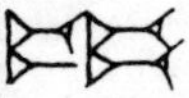	qu/qum		
91		kàs		
92	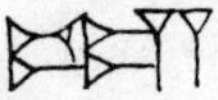	úr	ÚR = *sūnu* 'lap' = *pēnu* 'thigh'	

	I	II	III	IV
93		il		
94		du kup		
95		tum		
96			ANŠE = imēru 'donkey' 'a homer' (a measure) = determinative before equids and camels	 ANŠE.KUR.RA = sīsû 'horse'  EME = atānu 'jenny'
97			EGIR = (w)arki 'after'	
98	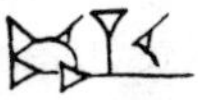			 GIŠ.GEŠTIN = ^{iš}karānu 'wine'
99		uš ús	NITA = zikaru 'male'	
100	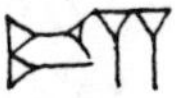	iš mil	SAḪAR = epru 'dust'	
101		bi pí kaš	KAŠ = šikaru 'beer'	
102	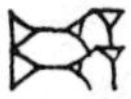	kib/p kep		
103	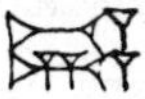		NA_4 = abnu 'stone' = determinative before stones	
104		qaq dà		
105	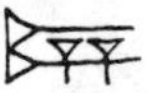	ni lí ṣal		 LÚ.Ì.DU_8 = ^{amēl}ātû 'gatekeeper'
106		e/ir		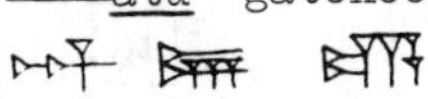 DINGIR.ERI.GAL = ^{d}Irkalla 'Irkalla'
107		mal		
108	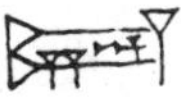		DAGAL = rapšu 'wide'	

	I	II	III	IV
109		daq ták		
110		pa ḫat		 GARZA = <u>parṣu</u> 'religious duty'  NA_4.PA = <u>aban</u><u>ayyartu</u> 'type of stone' 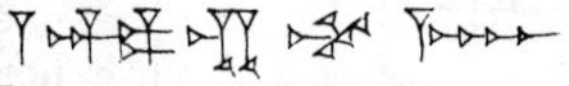 IDINGIR.MUATI.EN.MU.MEŠ = Id<u>Nabû</u>-<u>bēl</u>-<u>šumāti</u> 'Nabubel-shumati'
111	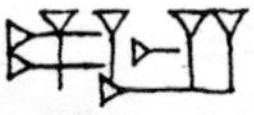	šab/p		
112		es/ṣ/z is/ṣ/z giš	GIŠ = <u>iṣu</u> 'wood' = determinative before trees and items made of wood	 GISSU = <u>ṣillu</u> 'shade'  $KIRI_6$ = <u>kirû</u> 'orchard' 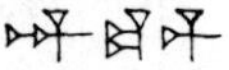 DINGIR.GIŠ.BAR = d<u>girru</u> 'fire'
113	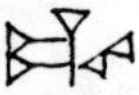		GUD = <u>alpu</u> 'ox'	
114		al		
115	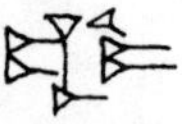	ár ub/p		
116	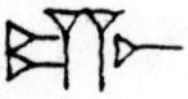	mar		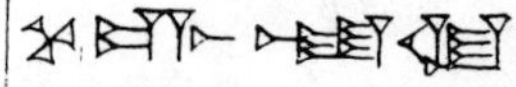 KUR.MAR.TU.KI = <u>māt</u><u>Amurri</u> 'West(land)'
117		e		
118	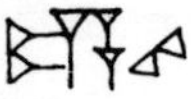	duk/q	DUG = <u>karpatu</u> 'pot' = determinative before pots and earthen containers	
119		un	UKU = <u>nišū</u> 'people'	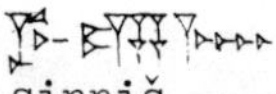 MÍ.UKU.MEŠ = <u>sinniš</u><u>sekrētu</u> 'concubines'
120	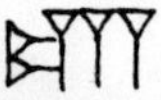	k/qit		
121	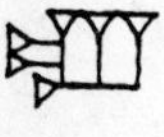	lak red rid šid šit		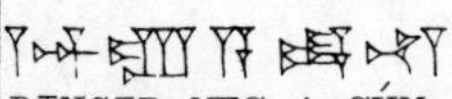 DINGIR.MES.A.SÚM-<u>na</u> = Id<u>Marduk</u>-<u>apla</u>-<u>iddina</u> 'Merodachbaladan'

	I	II	III	IV
122	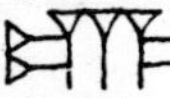	ú sam šam		
123	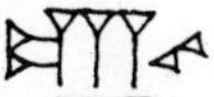	ga qá		
124		làḫ luḫ	SUKKAL = sukkallu 'vizier'	
125		dan kal lab reb rib	GURUŠ = eṭlu 'young man'	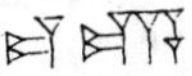 GIŠ.ESI = ^{iṣ}ušû 'ebony'
126				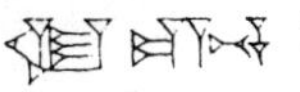 KARAŠ = karāšu 'camp'
127		é bit	É = bītu 'house'	 É.GAL = ēkallu 'palace'
128			GI_4 = târu 'to return'	
129	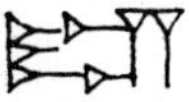	ra		
130	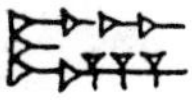		LÚ = awīlu/ amēlu 'man' = determinative before individuals	
131	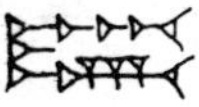		ŠEŠ = aḫu 'brother'	
132		šar		
133	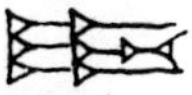	zak/q		
134		qar		
135		ed/t/ṭ id/t/ṭ		
136		lil		
137	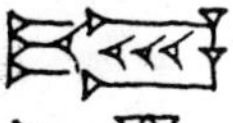		$MURUB_4$= qablu 'middle'	
138		d/ṭa		
139		ás áš		
140		ma		
141			GAL = rabû 'great'	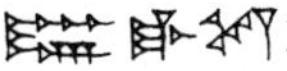 LÚ.TIRUM = ^{amēl}tīru 'courtier'

	I	II	III	IV
142		b/piš peš g/k/qir qer		
143		mir	AGA = <u>agû</u> 'crown'	 UKU.UŠ = <u>rēdû</u> 'soldier'
144		bur		
145		ša		
146		šu	ŠU = <u>qātu</u> 'hand'	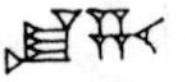 ŠU.ḪA = <u>bā'iru</u> 'soldier'
147		lib/p lul		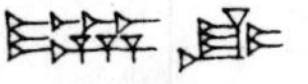 LÚ.NAR = <u>amēl</u><u>nāru</u> 'singer' 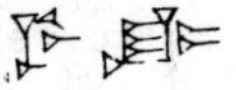 MÍ.NAR = <u>sinniš</u><u>nartu</u> 'female singer'
148		gam		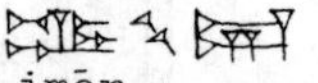 ANŠE.GAM.MAL = <u>imēr</u><u>gammālu</u> 'camel'
149		mat šad/t	KUR = <u>mātu</u> 'land' = <u>šadû</u> 'mountain' = <u>kašādu</u> 'to conquer' = determinative before lands	 KUR.NU.GI$_4$.A = <u>erṣet</u> <u>lā</u> <u>târi</u> 'land of no-return' = 'the netherworld'
150		še	ŠE = <u>še'u</u> 'grain'	
151		b/pu gít sír		
152	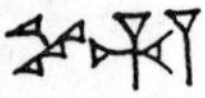	us/ṣ/z		
153	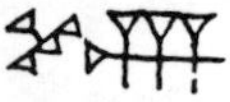	šud		
154		ṣir		
155		ter tir		
156		te		
157		kar	KAR = <u>kāru</u> 'town'	

	I	II	III	IV
158		liš		
159	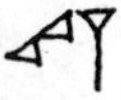	ud/t/ṭ ḫiš par per tam u_4	U_4 = ūmu 'day'	 ^{I}È-šu-na-mir = ^{I}Aṣûšunamir 'Asushunamir' 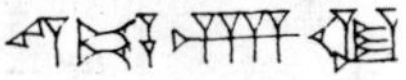 UD.KIB.NUN.KI = Sippar 'Sippar'  DINGIR.UTU = ^{d}Šamaš 'Shamash'
160		pi/e wa/e wi/u	GEŠTU = uznu 'ear'	
161		lìb	ŠÀ = libbu 'heart'	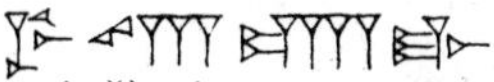 MÍ.ŠÀ.É.GAL = ^{sinniš}sekrētu 'concubines'
162	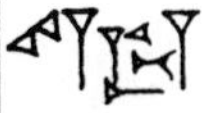	úḫ		
163			ERIM = ṣābu 'people'	 ERIM.ḪÁ = ummanāte 'army' 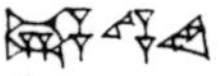 NA_4.NUNUZ = ^{aban}erimmatu 'egg-shaped bead'
164		zib		
165		ḫe/i ṭí		
166		a' e' i' u' 'a 'e 'i 'u		
167	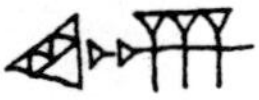	a/e/i ḫ uḫ		
168		kam	KAM = determinative after numbers	
169		e/im	IM = ṭiddu 'clay'	 IM.DUGUD = imbaru 'mist'
170		bir		
171		ḫar ḫur mur	ḪAR = šemīru 'bracelet'	 URU.ḪUR.SAG.KALAM.MA = ^{āl}Ḫursagkalamma 'Hursagkalamma'

	I	II	III	IV
172			ḪÁ = determinative after collectives	
173		u	10 = ešru 'ten'	12 = šinšer 'twelve'
174		muḫ	UGU = eli 'against', 'upon'	
175		lid		
176		kis/š		KIŠ.KI = Kiš 'Kish'
177		mi		
178		gul sún		
179				GIŠ.NÁ = [iṣ]eršu 'bed'
180		nim		KUR.ELAM.MA.KI = [māt]Elamtu 'Elam'
181		tùm		
182		lam		
183		ban		GIŠ.BAN = [iṣ]qaštu 'bow'
184		gim	GIM = kīma 'as', 'like'	
185		ul		
186			GÌR = šēpu 'foot'	LÚ.GÌR.NÍTA = [amēl]šakkanakku 'general', 'official'
187			GIG = murṣu 'disease'	
188		ši lim	IGI = īnu 'eye' 1000 = lim 'a thousand'	BAD_5.BAD_5 = dabdû 'defeat' IGI.SÁ = igisû 'gift'
189		ar		
190			SIG_5 = damqu 'good'	
191		ù		

	I	II	III	IV
192		d/ṭe d/ṭi		
193		ke/i qe/i	KI = erṣetu 'earth' = determinative after lands or places	KARAŠ = karāšu 'camp' MÍ.KI.SIKIL = ^{sinniš}wardatu 'young woman'
194		d/tin		
195		dun		
196				GUŠKIN = ḫurāṣu 'gold' KÙ.BABBAR = kaspu 'silver'
197		pat šuk		
198		man niš	20 = ešrā 'twenty'	
199		eš sin	30 = šalāšā 'thirty'	DINGIR.30 = ^{d}Sîn 'Sin'
200			50 = ḫanšā 'fifty'	
201		d/tiš	= ana 'unto' 1 = ištēn 'one' I = determinative before personal names 60 = šuššu 'sixty'	
202		gíl kil rim		
203				GIŠ.GIGIR = ^{iṣ}narkabtu 'chariot'
204		pul		
205		suk		
206		me šib šep	100 = me'at 'a hundred'	
207		míš	MEŠ = determinative af-	

	I	II	III	IV
			ter plurals and occasionally collectives	
208	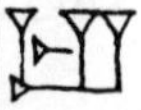	eb/p ib/p		
209		ku qú tuš	TUKUL = <u>tukultu</u> 'trust'	 GIŠ.TUKUL = <u>$^{iṣ}\text{kakku}$</u> 'weapon' GIŠ.TAKARIN = <u>$^{iṣ}\text{taskarinnu}$</u> 'box-wood' 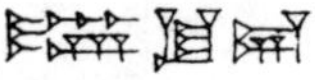 LÚ.ḪUN.GÁ = <u>$^{awīl}\text{agru}$</u> 'hired-man'
210	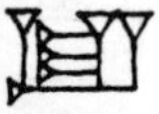	lu	UDU = <u>immeru</u> 'sheep'	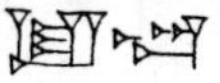 UDU.NÍTA = <u>immeru</u> 'sheep'
211	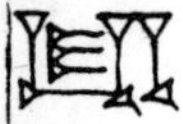	qe/i kin		
212		šú		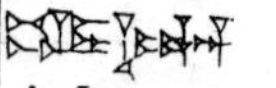 ANŠE.KUNGA = <u>$^{imēr}\text{parû}$</u> 'mule'
213		mim rak šal	MÍ = <u>sinništu</u> 'woman' =determinative before females	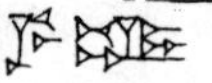 EME = <u>atānu</u> 'jenny'
214	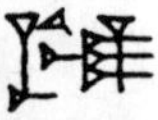	ṣu		
215	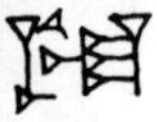	nin	NIN = <u>beltu</u> 'lady'	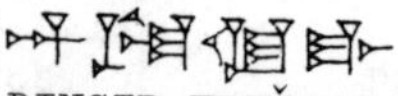 DINGIR.EREŠ.KI.GAL = <u>$^{d}\text{Ereškigal}$</u> 'Ereshkigal'
216	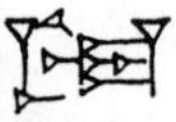	dam	DAM = <u>aššatu</u> 'wife'	
217		gu qù		 GIŠ.GU.ZA = <u>$^{iṣ}\text{kussû}$</u> 'seat'
218			GEME = <u>amtu</u> 'female-slave'	
219	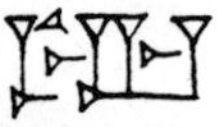	nik		
220	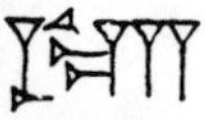	el		
221		lum		

	I	II	III	IV
222			2 = šinā 'two' = determinative after duals	
223		tuk/q		
224	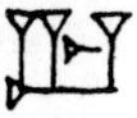	ur lik taš		
225		a	A = aplu 'heir' = mû 'water'	 A.ŠÀ = eqlu 'field' 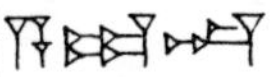 A.AB.BA = tâmtu 'sea'  A.RÁ = adi 'up to' 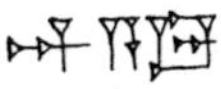 DINGIR.ÍD = ^{d}Id 'Rivergod'
226		ṣa za sà		
227		ḫa		
228		sik/q		
229			3 = šalāšu 'three'	
230		ṭu	GÍN = šiqlu 'shekel'	
231		šá	4 = erbu 'four' NINDA = akalu 'food'	 NÍG.GA = makkūru 'property'  NÍG.ŠU = bušû 'goods'
232		yá	5 = ḫamšu 'five'	
233		àš	6 = šeššu 'six'	
234			7 = sebû 'seven'	
235			8 = samānu 'eight'	

GLOSSARY

The meaning given to a word in the glossary is that which the particular word has in the context in which it is found. The citations refer to the first occurrence of a word in the texts. References to the Manual text are indicated by the symbol #. The numbers following CH refer to the laws of the Code of Hammurapi; those following Ish refer to lines of the Descent of Ishtar, while those following I, II, or III refer to lines of the columns of the Annals of Sennacherib. Root letters are given for all verbs with cross references as to exactly where a verb may be found in the glossary. Only verbs which appear in the texts in the I conjugation are listed with thematic vowels. However, different meanings are given where necessary for verbs which occur in other conjugations. Words written by means of a logogram are followed by the abbreviation 'w' (written), e.g., <u>kussû</u> w. GU.ZA 'seat'.

'

'bb	= e̲b̲ē̲b̲u̲
'br	= e̲b̲ē̲r̲u̲
abātu	IV/1 'to flee' II:14; #20.5
Abdili'ti	w. with I; 'Abdilit'ti' (from Arvad) II:52
abnu	w. NA$_4$ 'stone' I:30
abšānu	'rope' (of a yoke)
	+ š̲â̲ṭ̲u̲ 'to pull the ropes" II:68
abu	'father' CH 28
	w. AD Ish 83
	plural a̲b̲b̲ū̲ I:67
abullu	w. KÁ.GAL 'city gate' CH 15
adannu	'appointed time' CH 13
adāru (a̲, u̲)	I/1 'to fear' I:16
adi	'until' I:14
	'together with' I:21
	w. A.RÁ 'up to' CH 5
adû	p̲l̲u̲r̲a̲l̲e̲ t̲a̲n̲t̲u̲m̲ 'oath'
	b̲ē̲l̲ a̲d̲ê̲ u māmît 'vassal' II:74
agāru (a̲, u̲)	I/1 'to hire' CH 26
'gr	= a̲g̲ā̲r̲u̲
agru	w. LÚ.ḪUN.GÁ 'hired man' CH 26
agû	w. AGA 'crown' Ish 42
aḫātu	'sister'
	a̲ḫ̲ā̲t̲k̲i̲ (w. a̲ḫ̲ā̲t̲a̲k̲i̲) 'your sister' Ish 26
aḫu	'brother'
	plural a̲ḫ̲ḫ̲ū̲ w. ŠEŠ.MEŠ I:1
	w. PAP.MEŠ II:29
aḫu	'side' Ish 71
	i̲n̲a̲ a̲ḫ̲ī̲š̲a̲ 'alone' Ish 90

akālu (a, u)	I/1 'to eat' Ish 33
	w. KÚ Ish 19
akalu	'food' Ish 8
	w. NINDA.MEŠ Ish 33
Akkuddu	w. with URU; a city (of the Ellipi) II:16
Akkû	w. with URU; 'Akko' II:43
'kl	= akālu
akṣu	'dangerous' I:58
akû	'weak' I:6
Akzibi	w. with URU; 'Akzib' II:43
alaktu	'course' Ish 6
alāku (a, i)	I/1 'to go' CH 2
	'to flow' (tears) Ish 84
	infinitive CH 26; #11.3
	I/1, I/2 + ilku 'to perform corvée work' CH 27
	+ šimtu 'to die' CH 12
	III/1 adi lā bašî ušālik "I brought to naught" II:22; #20.7
alālu (a, u)	I/1 'to hang'
alpu	w. GUD 'ox' CH 7
	plural 'large cattle' I:51
'l'	= elû
'lk	= alāku
Altaqû	w. with URU; 'Eltekeh" II:82
ālu	w. URU 'city' CH 23
	mārē āli 'citizens' I:41
	plural ālānu I:36
am	ventive #4.11 - #4.13
'm'	= emû
amāru (a, u)	I/1 'to see' Ish 9
	'to examine' CH 9
amatu	'a word' Ish 13 = awatu #18.2

amměni	'why' Ish 43; #15.1
Amqarruna	w. with URU; 'Ekron' II:73
'mr	= amāru
amtu	w. GEME 'female slave' CH 7
Amurru	w. KUR.MAR.TU 'West' (land) II:58
ān	infix #8.6
'n'	= enû
ana	'unto' CH 2
	'for the purpose of' CH 3
	'up to' CH 13
anāku	'I' Ish 15; #13.7
āniš	adverbial ending #19.7
anni	direct suffix #15.2
annītu	feminine of annû 'this' Ish 28
	'behold' Ish 26; #14.11
annu	'crime' III:11; = arnu #21.4
annû	'this' Ish 28; #14.11
anum	adverbial ending #6.9
Anunnaki	netherworld deities Ish 32
anzillu	'abomination' II:77
aplu	w. A 'heir' in ^{Id}Marduk-apla-iddina
	'Merodachbaladan' I:20
appu	'nose' Ish 81
'pš	= epēšu
apsû	'deep water' Ish 27
aqru	'rare'
	feminine aqartu I:30
arammu	'ramp' III:21
Aramû	'Aramaeans' I:39
arāqu (i, i)	I/1 'to be yellow', 'to be green' Ish 29
'r'	= erû
'rb	= erēbu
ardatu	= wardatu
arḫiš	'quickly' II:71

arki	= warki
arnu	'penalty' CH 4
	+ bašû 'to commit a crime' III:13
'rq	= arāqu
Arrapḫa	w. with URU; 'Arrapha' II:6
'rš	= erēšu
âru	= wâru
arû	= warû
Arudāya	w. with URU; from Arvad II:52
Asdūdāya	w. with URU; from Ashdod II:54
Asdūdu	w. with URU; 'Ashdod' III:32
askuppatu	'threshold' Ish 107
	w. I.DIB Ish 112
'sr	= esēru
assinnu	'cult figure' Ish 92
'ṣ'	= waṣû
Aṣûšunamir	w. ^{I}È-šu-na-mir; name, lit. "His appearance is bright" Ish 92
'š'	= išû
ašar	conjunction 'where' Ish 8; #12.10
ašaredu	'foremost' I:8
ašru	'place' I:19
	'area' I:71
aššatu	w. DAM 'wife' II:62
Aššur	w. KUR.AŠŠUR.KI 'Assyria' I:2
atānu	w. EMÈ 'jenny' Ish 87
ātû	w. Ì.DU_8 'gatekeeper' Ish 13
'ṭ'	= eṭû
'ṭr	= eṭēru
awatu	'word' CH 3
awīlu	'a man' CH 1
Ayarammu	w. with I.DINGIR; name (from Edom) II:57
ayyartu	w. NA_4.PA 'type of stone' Ish 112
'zb	= ezēbu

'zr	= ezēru
Azūru	w. URU; 'Azuru' II:70

B

b'r	= bâru
babālu	by-form of wabālu
	bābil ḫiṭītu 'commiting a crime' III:12
Bābilu	w. KÁ.DINGIR.RA.KI 'Babylon' I:28
bābu	'gate' Ish 13
	w. KÁ Ish 12
baḫulātu	plurale tantum 'subjects', 'population' I:57
bā'iru	w. ŠU.ḪA 'soldier' CH 26
bakû (i, i)	I/1 'to weep' Ish 34
balāṭu	w. TI.LA 'life' Ish 114
baltu	'splendor' Ish 60 = baštu #16.6
balṭu	'living person' Ish 19
balṭussun	'alive' III:5; #21.3
balû	II/1 'to extinguish' CH 25
balu	'without' CH 7
Banāyabarqa	w. with URU; 'Banai-barqa' II:70
banû (i, i)	I/1, I/2 'to create', 'to fashion' Ish 91, 92
barāqu	III/1 'to strike with lightning' I:9
bâru	II/1 'to establish the true legal situation' CH 23
bašû (i, i)	I/1, IV/1 'to be' CH 5; I:34
	adi lā bašî alāku 'to come to naught' II:22; #20.7
	+ arnu 'to commit a crime' III:13
	III/1 + ḫiṭṭu 'to commit a crime' III:8-9
batāqu (a, u)	I/1 'to cut off' II:26

baṭiltu	'stoppage'
	iršû baṭlāti "refused to fight" (?) III:41
baṭlu	'interruption'
	lā baṭlu 'without interruption' II:49
beltu	'lady' Ish 23
	w. NIN Ish 44
bēlu	'owner' CH 9
	w. EN 'lord' I:36
	bēl adê u māmīt 'vassal' II:74
	bēl narkabti 'charioteer' III:3
	bēl pīḫāti 'commissioner' II:6
bēlūtu	'lordship' II:36
biltu	w. GUN 'tribute' I:31
	'talent' III:41
bīnu	w. with GIŠ; 'tamarisk' Ish 29
birītu	'clasp', 'fetter' II:75
birtūtu	*āl birtūti* 'fortified city' I:81
bītu	'house' 'estate' CH 9
	w. É CH 2
	bīt ṣēri 'tent' I:78
	bīt tuklāti 'stronghold' II:45
Bīt Ammanāya	w. KUR É.I.*Ammanāya*; from Beth Ammon II:55
Bīt Barrû	w. KUR.É.I.*Barrû*; region of the Ellipi II:25
Bīt Daganna	w. URU.É.*Daganna*; 'Beth Dagon' II:69
Bīt Kilamzaḫ	w. URU.É.I.*Kilamzaḫ*; city of the Kassites I:72
Bīt Kubatti	w. URU.É.I.*Kubatti*; city of the Kassites I:73
Bīt Zitti	w. URU.É.*Zitti*; 'Beth Zitti' II:42
bk'	= *bakû*
bl'	= *balû*
blkt	= *nabalkutu*

bn'	= banû
brq	= barāqu
bš'	= bašû
btq	= batāqu
bubūtu	'sustenance' Ish 8
burtu	'cow' Ish 77
bušû	w. NÍG.ŠU 'goods' I:30

D

d'k	= dâku
d'n	= dânu
dabdû	w. $BAD_5.BAD_5$ 'defeat' I:22
dadmû	'homes' I:17
dâku (a, u)	I/1 'to kill' CH 21
	IV/1 'to be executed' CH 1
dalāḫu (a, u)	I/1 'to stir up ' Ish 27
dalḫu	'turbid' Ish 33
daltu	'door' Ish 17
	w. GIŠ.IG Ish 11
damqu	feminine damiqtu 'good'
	damqātu 'good deeds' I:6
	w. SIG_5 in ṣābē damqūti 'best troops' III:39
Damunu	w. with LÚ; name of an Aramaean I:46
danānu	II/1 'to strengthen' III:39
	'to reinforce' I:82
dannatu	'fortress' CH 27
dannu	'strong' I:36
	'legitimate' I:2
dânu (a, i)	I/1 'to try a case' CH 5
dārišam	'for ever' I:64; #19:3
dayyānu	'judge' CH 5; #6.2
dayyānūtu	'judgeship' CH 5

dekû (i, i)	I/1 'to stir up' CH 11
dimtu	'tear'
	plural dīmā Ish 84
dimtu	'tower'
	plural dimātu III:9
dīnu	'case' CH 3
	'verdict' CH 5
ditallu	'ashes'
	ditalliš 'into ashes' I:79
dk'	= dekû
dlḫ	= dalāḫu
dnn	= danānu
dudittu	'(pectoral) ornament' Ish 51
dūru	w. BÀD 'city wall' Ish 106
	plural dūrānu I:36

E

ē	interjection 'no' Ish 99; #16.5
Ea	w. with DINGIR; the god Ea Ish 27
ebēbu	II/2 'to declare innocent' CH 2
ebēru	II/1 'to accuse' CH 1
ēdiš	'alone' I:19; #17.7
ēdu	'single person' I:59
Egalgina	place, lit. "palace of justice" Ish 111
ēkallu	w. É.GAL 'palace' CH 6
	mutabbillūt ēkalluš (instead of ēkallīšu or ekalliš, #17.6) 'his palace servants' I:33
Elamtu	w. ELAM.MA.KI 'Elam' I:21
elēnu	preposition 'above'
	elēnušša 'above her' (?) Ish 65; #15.12
elēnû	adjective 'upper'

	feminine elēnītu I:13
Elenzaš	w. with URU; city of the Ellipi II:27
eli	'against' CH 1
	'more than' Ish 20; #14.4
	w. UGU 'upon' Ish 11
	eli ša ūm pāni "more so than before" I:82
elippu	w. GIŠ.MÁ 'boat' CH 8
ellāmu	'front'
	ellāmū'a 'facing me' II:12
Ellipu	w. with KUR; land of the Ellipi II:11
elû (i, i)	I/1 'to go up' Ish 85
	III/1 'to raise up' Ish 19
emēdu (i, i)	I/1 'to impose' II:67
	+ šadû 'to disappear forever' II:40
emqu	'wise' Ish 91
emû	III/1 'to turn' I:78
emūqu	'power' I:35
	'army' II:80
enû (i, i)	I/1, I/2 'to change' CH 5
epēšu (e, u)	I/1 'to do' II:77
	+ pû 'to open the mouth' Ish 21
	+ usāti 'to give help' I:5
	II/1 'to treat' Ish 38
	III/1 'to have (a stela) made' II:7
epinnu	w. GIŠ.APIN 'plow'
	epinnēt āli 'city's gutters' Ish 104
epru	w. SAḪAR.ḪÁ 'dust' Ish 8
eqlu	w. A.ŠÀ 'field' CH 27
	eqel namraṣe 'difficult terrain' I:69
erbettu	w.  feminine of erbu 'four'
	kibrāt erbettim 'four regions', 'world' I:3; #17.2

erbû — w.  'four'
adi erbîšu 'up to fourfold' II:59

erēbu (u, u) — I/1 'to enter' Ish 5
ērunma Ish 25; #14.10
III/1 Ish 42

Ereškigal — w. DINGIR.Ereškigal; 'queen of the netherworld', lit. 'queen of the big place' Ish 1

erēšu (i, i) — I/1, I/2 'to request' Ish 102

erimmatu — w. NA_4.NUNUZ 'egg-shaped bead' Ish 48

erištu — 'a request' Ish 102

erṣetu — 'land' CH 23
w. KUR in erṣet lā târi, lit. "the land of no-return", "the land from which there is no return" = 'the netherworld' Ish 1
w. KI 'netherworld' Ish 44

eršu — w. GIŠ.NÁ 'bed' III:43

erû — III/1 'to impregnate' Ish 87

esēru (i, i) — I/1 'to imprison' III:29

eṣṣūru — 'bird' Ish 10
w. MUŠEN III:27

ešru — w.  'ten' CH 8

eššūtu — 'newness'
ana eššūti ṣabātu 'to reorganize' I:61; #19.1

eṭēru (i, i) — I/1 'to save' I:24

eṭlu — 'young man' Ish 79
'warrior' I:7
w. GURUŠ Ish 34

eṭû (i, i) — I/1 'to be dark' Ish 4

eṭûtu — 'darkness' Ish 9

ezēbu (i, i) — I/1 'to leave' Ish 34
izzibū (circumstantial clause, #14.7) I:17
III/1 'to have (a sealed document) made

	out' CH 5
ezēru (i, i)	I/1 'to curse' Ish 103

G

gabbu	'all' Ish 75
Gambulum	w. with LÚ; name of an Aramaean I:46
gammālu	w. ANŠE.GAM.MAL 'camel' I:52
gappu	= kappu
gašīšu	'stake' I:59
gillatu	'crime' III:11
gimirtu	'all' II:25
gimri	'all' I:11
girru	'campaign' I:20
girru	w. DINGIR.GIŠ.BAR 'fire' I:79
gitmālu	'perfect' I:7
Gublāya	w. with URU; from Byblos II:53
guḫlu	'antimony' III:42
gullultu	'crime' III:13
Gurumu	w. with LÚ; name of an Aramaean

Ḫ

ḫabannatu	w. with DUG; 'a container'
	ḫabannāt āli 'sewers of the city' Ish 105
ḫabātu (a, u)	I/1 'to rob' CH 22
	IV/1 'to be robbed' CH 23
ḫabbātu	'a robber' CH 23
ḫabtu	'robbed' CH 23
ḫadîš	'joyfully' I:28
ḫadû (u, u)	I/1 'to rejoice' Ish 41
Ḫagaranu	w. with LÚ; name of an Aramaean I:48
ḫā'iru	'husband' Ish 35

ḫalālu (a, u)	I/1 'to hang' CH 21
ḫalāqu (i, i)	I/1 'to lose' CH 9
	I/2 'to escape' CH 20
ḫalqu	'lost' CH 9
ḫalṣu	w. URU.ḪAL.ṢU 'fortification'
	+ rukkusu 'to erect a blockade' III:29
ḫalziqqu	w. with KUŠ; 'waterskin' Ish 98
Ḫamranu	w. with LÚ; name of an Aramaean I:48
ḫamšu	w. 𒐊 'five' CH 12
	'fifth' Ish 54
Ḫararāte	w. with URU; 'Harrutu' I:55
Ḫardišpi	w. with URU; city of the Kassites I:72
Ḫarḫar	w. with URU; 'Harhar' II:32
ḫarrānu	'expedition' CH 26
	'road' Ish 6
	+ ṣabātu 'to take the road' II:11
Ḫattu	w. with KUR; Hittite land II:37
Ḫazqia'u/ Ḫazqiya'u	w. with I; 'Hezekiah' (of Judea) II:76; III:18
Ḫaziti	w. with URU; 'Gaza' III:34
ḫbt	= ḫabātu
ḫd'	= ḫadû
Ḫindaru	w. with LÚ; name of an Aramaean I:47
Ḫirimme	w. with URU; 'Hirimmu' I:58
ḫirtu	'wife'
	plural ḫīrītu (for ḫīrātu) Ish 34
ḫiṭītu	'crime'
	bābil ḫiṭīti 'committing a crime' III:12
ḫiṭṭu	'crime' III:8
	bēl ḫiṭṭi 'rebel' I:42
ḫlq	= ḫalāqu
ḫubtu	'robbed thing' CH 22
ḫulqu	'lost property' CH 9

ḫurāṣu — w. GUŠKIN 'gold' CH 7

Ḫursagkalamma — w. with URU; 'Hursagkalamma' I:40

ḫuršānu — plurale tantum 'mountains' I:68

I

Id — w. DINGIR.ÍD 'River-god' CH 2

idû — I/1 'to know'
participle (irregular) mūdû CH 9

igisû — w. IGI.SÁ 'gift' II:58

ikkibu — 'forbidden thing'
utirra ikkibuš (< ikkibušu #17.6), lit. "I turned into his forbidden thing" = "I made it forbidden for him" III:30

ilku — 'corvée work'
+ alāku 'to perform corvée work' CH 27

ilu — 'god' CH 8
w. DINGIR CH 6
plural ilānu Ish 81; #16.1
w. DINGIR.MEŠ-ni I:63

imbaru — w. IM.DUGUD 'mist' II:15

imēru — w. ANŠE 'donkey' CH 7
'homer' (a measure) I:62; #19.2

immeru — w. UDU 'sheep' CH 7
w. UDU.NÍTA I:62

ina — 'in' CH 3
'from' CH 5
'within' CH 13
'through' I:35
'on' I:69
ina pāni 'before' CH 21
ina kašādīša "when she arrived" Ish 12; #13.1
ina lā ūmīšu 'prematurely' Ish 36

inṣabtu	'ring' Ish 45
īnu	'eye' CH 25
	w. IGI Ish 70
Irkalla	w. DINGIR.ERI.GAL 'netherworld' Ish 4 (for šarrat irkalli 'queen of the netherworld' ?)
irtu	w. GABA 'breast' Ish 51
Ispabāra	w. with LÚ; king of the Ellipi II:12
Išqalluna	w. with URU; 'Ashkelon' II:61
iš	adverbial ending #17.7
išam	adverbial ending #19.3
išātu	'fire' CH 25
Ištar	w. with DINGIR 'Ishtar' Ish 22
	w. INANNA Ish 2; #12.4
ištēn	w. 𒁹 'one' cardinal CH 24
	'first' ordinal Ish 42
ištu	w. TA 'from' preposition Ish 35
	'since' conjunction
	+ ullânumma 'no sooner than', 'scarcely' Ish 63; #15.11
išû (-, u/i)	I/1 'to have' CH 8; #8.7
itpēšu	'wise' I:3
itti	'with' CH 5
izru	'curse' Ish 103

K

k'l	= kâlu
k'n	= kânu
kabāsu	III/1 'to tramp down' III:21
kabattu	'liver'
	+ neperdû 'to be happy' Ish 96
	+ ušpardi 'to make happy' Ish 31; #15.4
kabittu	feminine of kabtu 'heavy' I:31

kadrû	'gift' II:67
kakku	w. GIŠ.TUKUL 'weapon' I:12
kal	'all' I:8
kalbannatu	'a siege engine' III:23
Kaldu	w. with KUR; 'Chaldea' I:37
Kaldû	w. with LÚ; 'Chaldean' I:39
kâlu	II/1 'to hold'
	feminine participle mukiltu ša keppê rabûti, lit. "the holder of the great skipping ropes" = "who holds the great skipping ropes" Ish 27
kalû (a, a)	I/2 'to confine' CH 19
kalû	'all' II:58; #20.8
Kammusunadbi	w. with I; name (from Moab) II:56
kânu	II/1 'to impose' I:64
	II/2 'to convict' CH 1
	'to prove' CH 3
kanāšu (u, u)	I/1 'to subdue' II:46
	I/2 'to submit' I:67
	III/1 'to bring to submission' I:15
kanšu	'submissive' I:49
kappu (gappu)	'wing'
	ṣubāt kappi 'plumage' Ish 10
karāšu	w. KARAŠ 'camp' I:23
karānu	w. GIŠ.GEŠTIN 'wine' I:62
karmu	'ruin'
	karmiš 'into a ruin' I:78
karru	'rags' Ish 82
kāru	w. URU.KAR 'town'
	in Kār-Sîn-aḫḫē-erība, new name of Elenzash, city of the Ellipi II:29
	in Kār-^{d}Dunyaš 'Babylon' I:21
kaspu	w. KÙ.BABBAR 'silver', 'money' CH 4

kašādu (a, u)	I/1 'to arrive' Ish 12
	'to conquer' I:27
	w. KUR-ud = akšud I:38; #18.9
	w. ak-šud^{ud} I:50
	I/2 'to reach' CH 27
	'to overcome' CH 2
Kaššû	w. KUR.LÚ.Kaššî; 'land of the Kassites' I:66
katāru (-, e)	I/1 'to make an alliance' II:81
kbs	= kabāsu
keppû	'skipping rope' Ish 27
kī'am	'thus' Ish 44
kibrātu	plurale tantum 'regions'
	kibrāt erbettim 'the world' I:3; #17.2
Kibrê	w. with LÚ; name of an Aramaean I:45
kīma	'as', 'like' Ish 29
	w. GIM Ish 10
	'instead of' Ish 33
kirû	w. $KIRI_6$ 'orchard' CH 27
Kiš	w. KIŠ.KI I:22
kišādu	w. GÚ 'neck' Ish 48
kišittu	'conquest' II:1
kišpū	plurale tantum '(charge of)sorcery' CH 2
kiššatu	'entire world' I:2
kittu	'right' I:4
kl'	= kalû
knš	= kanāšu
kšd	= kašādu
ktr	= katāru
kultāru	'tent' I:78
Kummaḫlum	w. with URU; city of the Ellipi II:23
kummu	'room' Ish 89
kunīnu	'bowl' or 'reed' Ish 30

kunukku 'sealed document' CH 5

kussû w. GIŠ.GU.ZA 'seat' CH 5
kussê nēmedi 'armchair' III:44

Kutâ w. GÚ.DU_8.A.KI; city I:41
name of the netherworld Ish 40

L

l'' = le'û

l'ṭ = lâṭu

lā 'not' CH 1; #3.11

labāšu (a, a) I/1 'to be clothed' Ish 10

labiru 'old' Ish 38

lakû 'weak' Ish 36

lamû (i, i) I/1 'to besiege' I:38 = lawû #18.2
III/1 'to encircle' I:60

lapan 'before' II:3

lâṭu (a, u) I/1 'to curb' I:8

lbš = labāšu

le'û (i, i) I/1 'to be able' CH 28

leqû (e, e) I/1 'to take' CH 9
I/2 CH 25

lētu 'cheek' Ish 108

libbu 'heart'
+ wabālu 'to want' Ish 31; #15.3
+ nâḫu 'to calm down', 'to become settled' Ish 96
ina libbi 'from it' Ish 99
'within' II:31
w. ŠÀ II:1

limētu 'environs' I:38

Li'tāu w. with LÚ; name of an Aramaean I:49

lītum 'victory' II:8

lm'	= lamû
lq'	= leqû
Lulî	w. with LÚ; king of Sidon II:38
lū	precative CH 9; #9.5
	asseverative I:68; #19.5
	coordinate conjunction CH 7; #8.1

M

m'd	= ma'ādu
ma	'and', 'but' CH 1
ma'ādu (i, a)	I/1 'to be numerous' Ish 20
Ma'bāya	w. with KUR; land of the Moabites II:56
Madāya	w. with KUR; land of the Medes II:33
magāru (a, u)	I/1 'to be submissive'
	lā māgirī 'the unsubmissive' I:9
Maḫalliba	w. with URU; 'Mahalliba' II:42
maḫāru (a, u)	I/1 'to receive' CH 6
maḫāṣu (a, a)	I/1 'to smite' Ish 17
	tamḫaṣ 3rd person feminine Ish 101; #16.7
	I/2 'to fight' III:2; #21.4
	'to attack' III:22
maḫru	'front', 'presence'
	ina maḫrīšunu 'before them' CH 9
	ina maḫrīya 'from me' Ish 114
	ana maḫrīya 'before me' II:59
	maḫar 'before' CH 9
maḫrû	'first' I:20; #15.8
	'former' II:29
	feminine maḫrītu III:35
makkūru	w. NÍG.GA 'property' CH 6
mala	'as much as' I:34; #18.4
Malaḫu	w. with LÚ; name of an Aramaean I:45

malāku — IV/1 'to think' Ish 65

malku — 'prince' I:8

maltītu — 'watering place' Ish 105; #16.6

malû — 'long hair' Ish 82

māmītu — 'oath'
bēl ādê u māmīt (for māmīti) 'vassal' II:74

mamman — 'whoever' #20.9
mamman lā 'no one' II:34

mandattu — 'tribute' II:35

manû (u, u) — I/1 'to count' I:35
+ ina qāt X "to put under the command of X" II:6-7

manû — w. MA.NA 'mina' (about 500 grams or 1 lb)
status absolutus mana CH 24; #8.3B

manzāzu — 'dwelling place' Ish 106
w. with LÚ; manzāz pāni 'royal attendant' I:32

maqātu — III/1 'to fall' I:58

Marduk-apla-iddina — w. DINGIR.MES.A.SÚM-na 'Merodachbaladan', king of Babylonia' I:20

martu — w. DUMU.MÍ 'daughter' Ish 2

Marubištu — w. with URU; city of the Ellipi II:16

māru — w. DUMU 'son' CH 7
māre āli 'citizens' I:41

maṣṣarūtu — 'safekeeping' CH 7

maṣû — II/2 'to strip off clothing' Ish 42

mašāru — II/1 'to abandon' I:26; #18.2

mašku — w. KUŠ 'hide'
mašak pīri 'elephant hide' III:44

mašqītu — 'watering place' II:45

mātu — w. KUR 'land' I:21
plural mātātu II:1

mē — poetic particle Ish 14; #13.4

melammû	'awe-inspiring luminosity' II:38
Meluḫḫi	w. with KUR; 'Ethiopia' II:80
mētiqu	'course' I:54
mgr	= *magāru*
mḫr	= *maḫāru*
mḫṣ	= *maḫāṣu*
mi	particle introducing direct quotations CH 9; #9.4
migru	'favorite' I:4
mimma	indefinite pronoun #8.2
	mimma šumšu 'anything' CH 7
mimmû	'property' CH 9
minâ	'what?' interrogative pronoun Ish 31; #15.1
Minḫimmu	w. with I; name II:50
mīnu	'number'
	ana lā mīnam 'without number' II:21; #20.6
miṣru	'territory' II:26
mīšaru	'justice' I:5
mitḫāriš	'all together' I:50; #17.7
Mitinti	w. with I; king of Ashdod II:54
mītu	'dead (person)' Ish 19
mlk	= *malāku*
mn'	= *manû*
mqt	= *maqātu*
mṣ'	= *maṣû*
mšr	= *mašāru*
mû	w. A.MEŠ *plurale tantum* 'water' Ish 32
mubbiru	'an accuser' CH 1
mūdû	I/1 (irregular) participle from *idû* 'to know'; 'one who knows' CH 9
mūdûtu	'knowledge' CH 9
munaggiru	'denouncer' CH 26
murṣu	w. GIG 'disease' Ish 70

musukkanu	w. with GIŠ; 'type of wood' (mulberry?) I:55
Muṣurāya	w. with KUR; 'Egyptian' III:4
Muṣuru	w. with KUR; 'Egypt'; II:78
mūšabu	'dwelling place' Ish 107
muškênu	w. MÁŠDA 'common citizen' CH 8
muttabbilu	'servant'
	muttabbilūt ēkalluš 'his palace servants' I:34; #18.5

N

n'ḫ	= nâḫu
nabalkutu	'to remove' Ish 18; #13.14
Nabatu	w. with LÚ; name of an Aramaean I:48
nabû (i, i)	I/2 'to name' II:30
Nabû-bēl-šumāti	w. I.DINGIR.MUATI.EN.MU.MEŠ governor of the city Harrate I:54
nadānu (i, i)	I/1 'to give', 'to pay' CH 5
	nadān šatti 'yearly tribute' III:35
	precative w. defectively lid<di>nūni Ish 99
	'to sell' CH 9
	w. SUM-na in ^{Id}Marduk-apla-iddina 'Merodachbaladan' I:20
	IV/1 innaddin CH 28; #11.7
nādinānu	'that seller' CH 9; #8.6
nadû (i, i)	I/1 'to hurl'
	'to bring' CH 1
	lā tanaddašši (expect tanaddîši direct suffix, #9.6) "don't throw it down" Ish 23
	IV/1 innaddi CH 25
nagāšu (i, i)	I/3 'to roam' I:71
nāgiru	'a herald' CH 16

nagû	'region' I:60
nâḫu (*a*, *u*)	I/1 'to calm down'
	+ *libbu* 'to be settled' Ish 96; #10.8
nakāru	II/1 'to change' II:29
nakru	w. LÚ.KÚR 'enemy' I:58
	nakriš 'like an enemy' II:77
namraṣu	'difficult' I:69
Namtar	w. with DINGIR; netherworld deity Ish 67
napāḫu	IV/1 'to break out' (fire) CH 25
napālu (*a*, *u*)	I/1 'to destroy' I:78
naparšudu	'to escape' I:24; #13.14
	ipparšiddū II:3; #20.2
napištu	'life' I:24
	dīn napištim 'capital case' CH 3
naqāru (*a*, *u*)	I/1 'to tear down'
narkabtu	w. GIŠ.GIGIR 'chariot' I:25
	narkabat šēpēya 'my own chariot' I:70
	bēl narkabti 'charioteer' III:4
nartu	w. MÍ.NAR 'female singer' I:33
nāru	w. LÚ.NAR 'singer'; I:32
narû	w. NA_4.RÚ.A 'a stela' II:7
nasāhu (*a*, *u*)	I/1 'to deport' II:64
naṣāru (*a*, *u*)	I/1 'to guard' I:4
našāku (*a*, *u*)	I/1 'to bite' Ish 101
našāqu (*i*, *i*)	I/1 'to kiss' II:60
našû (*i*, *i*)	I/1 'to raise' CH 25
	'to wear' Ish 82
	I/3 'to bear' CH 4
	III/1 'to have drawn up' I:70
nb'	= *nabû*
nblkt	= *nabalkutu*
nd'	= *nadû*
ndn	= *nadānu*

nēmedu	kussî nēmedi 'armchair' III:44
neperdû	'to be bright' #13.14
	I/1 + kabattu 'to be happy' Ish 96; #15.4
	III/1 + kabattu 'to make happy' Ish 31; #15.4
nertu	'murder charge' CH 1
ngr	= nagāru
ngš	= nagāšu
ni	direct suffix #9.6
	ventive ending #15.6
nibītu	'name' II:30
nību	'counting' I:77
	lā nībi 'innumerable' I:31
nigiṣṣu	'crevice' I:18
niksu	'cutting' Ish 29
	'breach' III:23
nim	ventive #15.6
Ninūa	w. NINA.KI 'Nineveh' III:47
Nippur	w. EN.LÍL.KI 'Nippur' I:40
nisiqtu	'precious' III:42
niṣirtu	'treasure' I:29
nīru	'yoke' II:36
	pān nīrīya utîr "I changed direction" II:10
nīšu	'life' CH 20
	w. MU Ish 97
	nīš ilim zakāru 'to swear by a god' CH 20; #10.7
nišū	'people' CH 24
	w. UKU.MEŠ I:50
nkr	= nakāru
nks	= nakāsu
npḫ	= napāḫu
npl	= napālu

nprd	= neperdû
npršd	= naparšudu
nqr	= naqāru
nsḫ	= nasāḫu
nṣr	= naṣāru
nš'	= našû
nšk	= našāku
nšq	= našāqu
numātu	'furnishings' CH 25
nūru	'light' Ish 7

P

Padî	w. with I; king of Ekron II:74
pagru	'corpse' I:59
palāḫu (a, a)	I/1 'to fear' II:78
palāšu (a, u)	I/1 'to break (into a house)' CH 21
pānû	'face' Ish 29
	+ šakānu 'to proceed' Ish 93; #16.4
	ina pāni 'before' CH 21
	eli ša ūm pāni 'more so than before' I:82
	pān nīrīya utîr "I changed direction" II:10
	manzāz pāni 'royal attendant' I:32
Papsukkal	w. with DINGIR; name of vizier Ish 81
parāsu (a, u)	I/1 'to render (a decision)' CH 5
	+ warkatu 'to investigate the circumstances of a case' IV/1 CH 18
parakku	'dais'
	āšib parakki 'king' I:12
parāšu	IV/1 'to flee' I:19
parṣu	w. GARZA 'religious duty' Ish 38
parû	w. ANŠE.KUNGA 'mule' I:25
parzillu	w. AN.BAR 'iron' II:75

pašaqu	III/1 'to be most difficult' I:71; #19.6
pāṭu	'territory' CH 23
pēnu	w. ÚR 'thigh' Ish 101
petû (i, i)	I/1, I/2 'to open' Ish 14, 39
	petašši 'open for her' Ish 37
	IV/1 'to be opened' Ish 94
piḫātu	'district'
	w. LÚ.EN.NAM bēl piḫāti 'commissioner' II:6
pilšu	'breach' CH 21
	'tunnel' III:23
pīru	w. AM.SI 'elephant'
	mašak pīri 'elephant hide' III:44
plḫ	= palāḫu
plš	= palāšu
prs	= parāsu
prš	= parāšu
pršd	= naparšudu
pt'	= petû
Pūdu-ili	w. with I; name II:55
puḫru	'assembly' CH 5
pūḫu	'substitute' CH 26
pulḫū	plurale tantum 'terror' II:38
Puqudu	w. with LÚ; name of an Aramaean I:47
purussû	'decision' CH 5
pû	'mouth' Ish 21

Q

qablu	w. $MURUB_4$ 'hip' Ish 54
	'into' II:40
	ina qabal 'in the middle of' I:23
qabû (i, i)	I/1, I/2 'to speak' CH 3, CH 9
	I/1 stative 'was commanded' CH 26

qadādu	II/1 'to hang down' Ish 81
qamû (-, *u*)	I/1 'to burn' I:79
qaqqadu	w. SAG.DU 'head' Ish 42
	ṣalmāt qaqqadi 'mankind' I:15
qaqqaru	'land' Ish 1
qardu	'strong' I:7
qaštu	w. BAN 'bow'
	ṣābe qašti 'bowmen' II:79
qātu	'hand' CH 6
	w. ŠU Ish 57
	ina qāti 'from' CH 6
	ina qāt X manû 'to put under the command of' II:6-7
qb'	= *qabû*
qdd	= *qadādu*
qerbu	'midst' I:27
qerēbu (*i*, *i*)	I/1 'to draw near' CH 13
	+ *ana* 'to assault' III:7
qīpu	w. with LÚ 'governor' I:55
qitrubu	'onslaught' I:26; #18.1
qm'	= *qamû*
qrb	= *qerēbu*
quppu	'cage' III:27

R

r'b	= *râbu*
r'm	= *râmu*
r'š	= *rêšu*
rabi'ānu	'mayor' CH 23
râbu (*a*, *i*)	I/1 'to compensate' CH 8; #8.8
	'to substitute' in *Sîn-aḫḫē-erība* 'Sennacherib' I:1
	w. SU II:29

râbu (u, u)	I/1 'to tremble', 'to shake with fear' Ish 64
rabû	II/1 'to rear' CH 29
	III/1 'to make great' I:12
rabû	'great', 'old'
	w. GAL-ti feminine rabīti Ish 22
	plural rabûtu Ish 27
	status absolutus ṣeḫer rabi 'young and old' I:50; #17.4
radû	II/1 'to add to' II:27
rakābu (a, a)	I/1 'to ride' I:69
rakāsu	II/1 + ḫalṣī 'to erect blockades' III:29
rakbu	'messenger' III:49
râmu (a, a)	I/1 'to love' I:5
ramû	III/1 + šubtu 'to settle somebody' II:5 #20.3
rapāšu	II/1 'to enlarge' II:32
rappu	'bridle' I:8
rapšu	feminine rapaštu 'wide'
	w. DAGAL II:15
raqû (i, i)	I/2 'to hide' CH 16
rašubbātu	plurale tantum 'terror' II:45
rašû (i, i)	'to have'
	iršū baṭlāti 'they refused to fight' (?) III:41
rb'	= rabû
rd'	= radû or redû
rē'û	'shepherd' I:3
rebû	w.  'fourth' Ish 51; #15.8
redû (i, i)	I/1, I/2 'to lead' CH 17; CH 18
	+ am 'to produce' CH 13
rēdû	w. UKU.UŠ 'soldier' CH 26
rēṣu	'helper' I:22

rēṣūtu	'assistance' II:81
	rēṣussun 'to their assistance' #21.3
reštu	'choice' I:63
rēšu	w. SAG 'head' Ish 98
	šūt rēši 'commander' II:6; #20.4
rêšu (e, e)	I/1 'to rejoice' Ish 40
Riḫiḫu	w. with LÚ; name of an Aramaean I:44
rikistu	'contract'
	plural riksātu CH 7
rīmu	'wild bull'
	rīmāniš 'like a wild bull' I:71; #19.7
rītu	'pasture' II:44
rkb	= rakābu
rks	= rakāsu
rm'	= ramû
rpš	= rapāšu
rq'	= raqû
rš'	= rašû
Ru'ūa	w. with LÚ; name of an Aramaean I:47
rubû	w. LÚ.NUN 'prince' II:73
rugummû	'claim' CH 5
Rukibti	w. with I; king of Ashkelon II:65
ruqqu	see rūqu
rūqu	'far' II:39
	plural rūqūtu 'far away places' II:33
	rūqētu II:14

S

saḫāpu (a, u)	I/1 'to envelope' II:15
saḫāru (u, u)	I/1 'to surround'
	sāḫiru damqāti 'who does good deeds' I:6 #17.3
salāḫu (a, u)	I/1 'to sprinkle' Ish 114

Samsimurunāya	w. with URU; from Samsimuruna II:50
sandu	w. NA_4.AN.GUG.ME 'red' III:43
sarrātu	'falsehood'
	šībūt sarrātim 'false testimony' CH 3
sarru	'liar' CH 11
sebet	w.  'seven' cardinal
	sebet bābi 'seven gates' Ish 94
sebû	w.  'seventh' ordinal Ish 60
sekrētu	w.MÍ.ŠÀ.É.GAL 'concubines' I:31
	w. MÍ.UK̀U.MEŠ III:46
sḫp	= saḫāpu
sḫr	= saḫāru
sidru	'battle line' II:83
siḫirti	'all' I:33
	siḫirti āli 'all round the city' I:60
sikkūru	'lock' Ish 17
	w. GIŠ.SAG.KUL Ish 11
Sîn	w. DINGIR.30 'Sin' Ish 2; #12.4
	w. DINGIR.EN.ZU I:1; #17.1
Sîn-aḫḫē-erība	w. I.DINGIR.ZU.EN.ŠEŠ.MEŠ-eri-ba
	'Sennacherib' I:1
	w. I.DINGIR.30.PAP.MEŠ.SU II:29
sinništu	w. MÍ 'female'
	zikar u sinniš 'male and female' I:51; #17.4
Sippar	w. UD.KIB.NUN.KI 'Sippar' I:41
sippu	'door jamb' Ish 18
sīsû	w. ANŠE.KUR.RA 'horse' I:25
sittu	'rest'
	plural sittûtu III:12
slḫ	= salāḫu
sukkallu	w. SUKKAL 'vizier' Ish 67
suluppu	w. ZÚ.LUM.MA 'date' I:62

sūnu	w. ÚR 'lap' Ish 35
sutinnu	w. with MUŠEN following; 'bat' I:18
sūqu	w. SILA 'street' Ish 78

Ṣ

ṣabātu (*a*, *a*)	I/1, I/2 'to seize' CH 9
	+ *ana* *eššūti* 'to reorganize' I:61; #19.1
	+ *ḫarrānu* 'to take the road' II:11
	IV/2 'to have been captured' CH 19
ṣābitānu	'that captor' CH 20; #8.6
ṣābu	w. LÚ.ERIM 'soldier'
	ṣābē *qašti* 'bowmen' II:79
ṣalāmu (*i*, *i*)	I/1 'to become black' Ish 30
ṣalmu	'black'
	ṣalmāt *qaqqadi*, lit. 'black ones of the head' = 'mankind' I:15
ṣamû	II/1 'to thirst' > 'to lack'
	stative masculine plural *ṣummû* *nūra* "they are deprived of light" Ish 7
ṣamû	'thirsty' Ish 108
Ṣariptu	w. with URU; 'Zaribtu' II:42
ṣbt	= *ṣabātu*
ṣeḫēru (*i*, *i*)	I/1 'to be young' CH 29
	II/1 'to diminish' II:22
ṣeḫru	'young', 'small' CH 14
	w. TUR II:41
	status *absolutus* *ṣeḫer* *rabi* 'young and old' I:50; #17.4
ṣēnu	'small cattle' I:52
ṣēru	'field' CH 17
	w. EDIN in *bīt* *ṣēri* 'tent' I:78
ṣēru	'back'
	ṣēruššu (< *ṣērumšu*) 'upon it' II:9;#17.5

	'on him' II:49
ṣḫr	= ṣehēru
Ṣidqa	w. with I:king of Ashkelon II:60
Ṣidunnāya	w. with URU; 'Sidonite' II:51
Ṣidunnu	w. with URU; 'Sidon' II:38
Ṣilli-bēl	w. I.GISSU.EN; name III:33
ṣillu	w. GISSU 'shade' Ish 106
Ṣisirtu	w. with URU; city of the Ellipu II:23
ṣītu	'going out'
	ṣīt šamši 'east' I:14
ṣlm	= ṣalāmu
ṣm'	= ṣamû
ṣubātu	'garment'
	ṣubāt balti 'robe of splendor' Ish 60
	ṣubāt kappi 'plumage' Ish 10
ṣumbu	w. with GIŠ; 'wagon' I:25

Š

š'l	= šêlu
š'm	= šâmu
š'ṭ	= šâṭu
ša	relative pronoun 'who', 'which', 'what' CH 2; #6.16
	genitive indicator 'of' CH 8; #8.5
šabāḫu	
	šabuḫ epru 'dust is poured out' Ish 11
	unusual, epect epru tabik/šapik/nadi
šadlu	'wide'
	igisê šadlūti 'rich offerings' II:58
šadû	w. KUR 'mountain' I:10
	+ emēdu 'to disappear' II:40
šaḫāṭu (i, i)	I/1 'to mount' Ish 77
šaḫû	w. ŠAḪ 'pig' CH 8

šakānu (a, u)	I/1 'to set' CH 13
	+ uznu 'to direct one's attention' Ish 2 #12.5
	+ pānû 'to proceed' Ish 93; #16.4
	I/2 + dabdû 'to defeat' I:22
	I/3 II:9
šakkanakku	w. LÚ.GÌR.NÍTA 'general', 'official' II:73
šakru	'drunken' Ish 108
šalālu (a, u)	I/1 'to take as spoil' I:38
	stative feminine plural šallū (for šallā) Ish 35
šalāmu (i, i)	I/2 'to be safe' CH 2
	šalām šamši 'west' I:13
šalāšā	w. 𒌍 'thirty' CH 8
šallatu	'spoil'
	šallatiš 'as spoil' I:35; #17.7
šalšu	'third' II:37
	w. 𒐈 Ish 48
	feminine šaluštu CH 29
šalû (i, i)	I/1 'to plunge into' CH 2
šamšu	w. DINGIR.UTU 'Shamash' Ish 83
	'the sun' I:13
šâmu (a, a)	I/1, I/2 'to purchase' CH 7, CH 9
	IV/1 CH 9
šanānu (a, u)	I/1 'to rival'
	lā šanān 'unrivaled' I:10; #17.4
šanû	II/1 'to tell', 'to inform' Ish 24
šanû	'another' CH 27
	w. 𒈫 'second' Ish 45
šapāru (a, u)	I/1 'to send' III:49
šaplû	'lower'
	feminine šaplītu I:14
šaptu	'lip' Ish 30
	plural šapātūša 'her lips' Ish 30

šaqālu (a, u)	I/1 'to pay' CH 9
šaqû	II/1 'to raise' Ish 98
šarāqu (i, i)	I/1 'to steal' CH 6
	I/2 'to kidnap' CH 14
šarrāqānu	'that thief' CH 8; #8.6
šarrāqu	'thief' CH 7
šarratu	'queen' Ish 24
šarru	'king' CH 26
	w. LUGAL Ish 84
Šarru-lū-dāri	w. I.LUGAL-lū-dāri; king of Ashkelon II:65
šarrūtu	w. LUGAL-ut 'kingship' I:10
	bīt šarrūti 'capital city' II:17
šâšu	independent dative pronoun 'to him' #13.7
	used as accusative II:61
šattu	'year'
	šattišam 'yearly' II:49
	nadān šatti 'yearly tribute' III:35
šatû (i, i)	I/1 'to drink' Ish 32
	lultati Ish 99; #16.6
šaṭāru	III/1 'to have inscribed' II:9
šâṭu (a, u)	I/1 'to pull' II:68
šayyāmānu	'that buyer' CH 9; #8.6
šb''	= šubê'u
šbḫ	= šabāḫu
šbr	= šebēru
še'u	w. ŠE 'grain' CH 4
šebēru (i, i)	I/1 'to break' Ish 17
šêlu	II/1 'to sharpen' III:1
šemiru	'ring' Ish 120
	w. ḪAR Ish 57
šemû (i, i)	I/1 'to hear' Ish 28
	'to obey' II:34
šepṣu	'powerful' I:16

šēpu	w. GÌR 'foot' Ish 57
	šēpū'a 'at my feet' I:15; #17.5
	narkabat šēpēya 'my own chariot' I:70
	zūk šēpi 'infantry' III:22
šerru	w. LÚ.BÀNDA 'child' Ish 36
šeššu	w. 𒐋 'six' CH 13
	'sixth' Ish 57
šḫṭ	= šaḫāṭu
šibbu	'girdle' Ish 54
šību	'witness' CH 7
šībūtu	'testimony' CH 3
šikaru	w. KAŠ.MEŠ 'beer' Ish 33
šimtu	'fate'
	ana šimti ittalak 'to die' CH 12; #9.8
šīmu	'purchase' CH 9
šinā	w. 𒈫 'two' CH 17
šinnu	w. ZU 'ivory' III:43
šinšer	w. 𒌋𒈫 'twelve' CH 5
šiqlu	w. GÍN 'shekel'; CH 17
šisītu	'summons' CH 16
škn	= šakānu
šl'	= šalû
šll	= šalālu
šlm	= šalāmu
šm'	= šemû
šn'	= šanû
šnn	= šanānu
špr	= sapāru
šq'	= šaqû
šql	= šaqālu
šrq	= šarāqu
št'	= šatû
šṭr	= šaṭāru

<u>šu</u>	direct suffix #9.6
	as multiplicator with <u>i</u> #6.17
<u>šû</u>	independent pronoun 'he' III:37; #13.7
	demonstrative 'that' CH 3
<u>šu'āti</u>	independent accusative/genitive pronoun #13.7
	demonstrative 'that' CH 2
<u>šubê'u</u>	'to rush', 'to dash out' Ish 65; #15.12
<u>šubtu</u>	'dwelling' Ish 4
<u>šum</u>	indirect suffix #9.6
<u>šumma</u>	'if', 'when' conjunction CH 1
<u>šumu</u>	'name' CH 7; #8.2
	w. MU Ish 24
<u>šupšuqu</u>	'most difficult' I:71; #19.6
<u>šupû</u>	'battering ram' III:22
<u>šurqu</u>	'stolen (property)' CH 6
<u>šuššu</u>	'sixty' Ish 69
<u>šūt</u>	plural of <u>ša</u> #20.4

<u>T</u>

<u>t'r</u>	= <u>târu</u>
<u>tabālu</u> (<u>a</u>, <u>a</u>)	I/1, I/2 'to take away' CH 2, Ish 42
<u>tāḫāzu</u>	'battle' I:16
<u>takālu</u>	II/1 'to encourage' I:65
<u>takkassu</u>	'stone block' III:43
<u>talāmu</u>	III/1 'to bestow on', 'to confer' I:11
<u>tamḫāru</u>	'battle' I:23
<u>tāmartu</u>	'tribute' I:57
<u>tamirtu</u>	'outskirts' I:22
<u>Tamnâ</u>	w. with URU; 'Timnah' III:6
<u>tâmtu</u>	'sea' II:40
	w. A.AB.BA I:13
<u>tamû</u>	II/1 'to make swear' Ish 97

tappūtu	'aid' I:6
târu (a, u)	I/1, I/2 'to return' CH 5, CH 27
	w. GI_4 in KUR.NU.GI_4.A = erṣet lā târi 'land of no-return' = 'land from which there is no return', 'the netherworld' Ish 1
	II/1 'to turn', 'to return to' CH 18
	pān nīrīya utîr "I changed direction" II:10
	utirra ikkibuš "I made it forbidden for him" III:30
	stative 'was taken captive' CH 27
	II/2 Ish 119
taskarinnu	w. TASKARIN 'box-wood' III:45
tayyartu	'return' I:43
tb'	= tebû
tbl	= tabālu
tebû	III/1 'to remove' CH 5
tikku	'neck' I:70
tīru	w. LÚ.TIRUM 'courtier' I:32
tkl	= takālu
tlm	= talāmu
tm'	= tamû
Tu'mūna	w. with LÚ; name of an Aramaean I:43
Tuba'lum	w. with I; name II:47
tukultu	w. TUKUL 'trust' III:1
	bīt tuklāti 'stronghold' II:45
tuššu	'calumny', 'slander' CH 11

Ṭ

ṭarādu (a, u)	I/1 'to drive off' Ish 36
	I/2 'to send away' CH 26
ṭiddu	'clay' Ish 8
	w. IM Ish 33

ṭrd	= *ṭarādu*

U

u	'and', 'or' CH 4
ubānu	'finger' Ish 101
Ubudu	w. with LÚ; name of an Aramaean I:44
Ubulum	w. with LÚ; name of an Aramaean I:46
Udummāya	w. with KUR; Edomite II:57
ul	'not' CH 5
ullânumma	'before'
	ištu ullânumma 'no sooner than', 'scarcely' Ish 63; #15.11
	ultu ullânumma 'ever since' Ish 86
ullâ	
	ultu ullâ 'since time immemorial' I:67
ultu	preposition 'from' Ish 96
	w. TA Ish 35
	conjunction *ultu ullânumma* 'ever since' Ish 86; #15.11
um	adverbial ending #17.5
ummānu	w. ERIM
	plural *ummānātu* 'army' I:21
ummânu	'artisan' I:33
ummu	'mother' CH 29
ūmu	w. U_4 'day'
	ina lā ūmīšu 'prematurely' Ish 36
	eli ša ūm pāni 'more so than before' I:82
unūtu	'utensil' I:29
urbi	w. with LÚ; type of warrior I:39
Ursalimmu	w. with URU; 'Jerusalem' III:15
Uruk	w. UNU.KI 'Uruk' I:40
Urumilki	w. with I: name (from Byblos) II:53
usātu	'help'

	ēpis usāti 'who gives help' I:5
usû	w. GIŠ.ESI 'ebony' III:45
Ušû	w. with URU; 'Ushu' II:43
utūlu	'to lie down' Ish 79; #16.2
ūtu	abstract ending #4.3
uznu	'ear' Ish 98
	w. GEŠTU Ish 45
	+ šakānu 'to direct one's attention' Ish 2; #12.5
uzuzzu	'to stand' Ish 23; #14.9
	III/1 ulziz (< ušziz #16.6) II:10

W

w'r	= wâru
wabālu (a, i)	I/1 'to bring' CH 9
	+ libbu 'to want' Ish 31; #15.3
	III/1 'to send' III:48
warādu (a, i)	I/1 'to go down' Ish 63
	III/1 'to bring down' II:4
wardatu	w. MÍ.KI.SIKIL 'young woman' Ish 35; #12.7
wardu	w. ÌR 'slave' CH 7; #12.7
wardūtu	w. ÌR-ūtu 'obesience' III:49; #12.7
warḫu	w. ITU 'month' CH 13
warka	'afterwards' CH 19
warkânu	'afterwards' CH 5
warki	'after' Ish 76; #12.7
	warkīšu 'after him' CH 27; #11.4
	w. EGIR III:48
warkatu	
	+ parāsu 'to investigate the circumstances of a case' CH 18
wâru (i, i)	I/1 'to go'
	ašar lā âri 'inaccessible land' I:19; #12.7

warû (*u*, *u*)	I/1 'to lead', 'to bring' II:64
waṣû (*i*, *i*)	I/1 'to go out' CH 3; #12.7
	III/1 'to strike' Ish 69
	'to bring out' Ish 113
	III/2 'to let escape' CH 15
wašābu (*a*, *i*)	I/1 'to sit', 'to dwell' CH 5; #12.7
	āšib parakki 'king' I:12
	III/1 Ish 113
	'to repopulate' II:1
wašāru	II/1 'to release' III:14; #18.2
	II/2 'to set free' CH 20
wbl	= *wabālu*
wld	= *walādu*
wr'	= *warû*
wrd	= *warādu*
wṣ'	= *waṣû*
wšb	= *wašābu*
wšr	= *wašāru*

Y

Yadaqqu	w. with LÚ; name of an Aramaean I:44
Yappû	w. with URU; 'Joppa' II:69
yaraḫḫu	w. NA_4.TU 'ruby' (?) Ish 54
Yasubigallāya	w. with KUR.LÚ; from Yasubigalla I:66
Yaudāya	w. with KUR; 'Judaean' II:76

Z

z'n	= *zânu*
zakāru (*a*, *u*)	I/1, I/2 'to speak' Ish 13
	I/2 'to name' CH 18
	+ *nīš ilim* 'to swear' CH 20; #10.7

zāmânu	'enemy' I:9
zânu	II/1 'to overlay', 'to stud with precious stones' Ish 116
	For za'ina in Ish 112 read zu''in
zaqru	'steep' I:68
zēru	w. NUMUN 'seed' II:63
zikaru	'warrior' I:7
	w. NITA in zikar u sinniš 'male and female' I:51; #17.4
zikru	'idea' Ish 91
	'mention' II:35
	w. MU 'name' Ish 24
zkr	= zakāru
zūku	
	zūk šēpi 'infantry' III:22
zumru	'body' Ish 60

INDEX

SUGGESTIONS FOR FURTHER READING

For students interested in pursuing further studies in Akkadian language and literature the following is a brief listing of some selected books and articles.

Sign Lists

R. Borger, *Akkadische Zeichenliste* (Neukirchen-Vluyn, 1971).

R. Labat, *Manuel d'épigraphie akkadienne* (Paris, 1963), revised edition 1976 by F. Malbran-Labat.

Dictionaries

AHw. = W. von Soden, *Akkadisches Handwörterbuch* (Wiesbaden, 1959-), 14 fascicles published to date, from *a* to *tēšû*.

CAD = I. J. Gelb, A.L. Oppenheim, *et al*., *The Assyrian Dictionary of the Oriental Institute of the University of Chicago* (Chicago & Gluckstadt, 1956-), 13 volumes published to date: *A*[1], *A*[2], *B*, *D*, *E*, *G*, *Ḫ*, *I/J*, *K*, *L*, *M*, *Ṣ*, *Z*.

Grammars

W. von Soden, *Grundriss der akkadischen Grammatik*, and *Ergänzungheft zum Grundriss*, Analecta Orientalia 33/47 (Rome, 1969).

A. Ungnad & L. Matouš, *Grammatik des Akkadischen* (Munich, 1964).

Textbooks

T. Bauer, *Akkadische Lesestücke* (Rome, 1953).

R. Borger, *Babylonisch-assyrische Lesestücke* (Rome, 1963).

K. Riemschneider, *Lehrbuch des Akkadischen* (Leipzig, 1969), translated into English by T. A. Caldwell, J. N. Oswalt, & J. F. X. Sheehan (Marquette University, 1974).

Some Transliterated Text Editions

Myths and Epics

R. Borger, "Die Höllenfahrt der Göttin Ištar" in *Babylonisch-assyrische Lesestücke*, vol. 2, 86-93.

R. Labat, *Le poème babylonien de la création* (*Enūma eliš*) (Paris, 1935).

W. G. Lambert & A. R. Millard, *Atra-ḫasīs The Babylonian Story of the Flood* (Oxford, 1969).

R. C. Thompson, *The Epic of Gilgamish* (Oxford, 1930).

Legal Texts

G. R. Driver & J. C. Miles, *The Assyrian Laws* (Oxford, 1935).

G. R. Driver & J. C. Miles, *The Babylonian Laws* (Oxford, 1952 & 1955).

A. Goetze, *The Laws of Eshnunna*, Annual of the American Schools of Oriental Research 31 (New Haven, 1956).

D. J. Wiseman, *The Vassal-Treaties of Esarhaddon* (London, 1958).

Letters

G. Dossin, *Correspondence de Šamši-Addu*, Archives royales de Mari 1 (Paris, 1950).

F. R. Kraus, *Altbabylonische Briefe aus dem British Museum* (Leiden, 1964).

S. Parpola, *Letters from Assyrian Scholars to the Kings Esarhaddon and Assurbanipal* (Neukirchen-Vluyn, 1970).

A. F. Rainey, *El Amarna Tablets* (Neukirchen-Vluyn, 1970).

Prayers and Incantations

E. Ebeling, *Die akkadische Gebetsserie "Handerhebung"* (Berlin, 1953)

W. G. Lambert, "The Shamash Hymn" in *Babylonian Wisdom Literature* (Oxford, 1960), 121-38.

G. Meier, *Die assyrische Beschwörungssamlung Maqlû* (Osnabrück, 1967).

E. Reiner, *Šurpu, A Collection of Sumerian and Akkadian Incantations*

(Graz, 1958).

Royal Inscriptions

R. Borger, Die Inschriften Asarhaddons Königs von Assyrien (Osnabrück, 1967).

R. Borger, "Zwei Königsinschriften Samsuiluna's von Babylon" in Babylonisch-assyrische Lesestücke, vol. 2, 47-49.

L. W. King, The Letters and Inscriptions of Hammurabi (London, 1900).

D. D. Luckenbill, The Annals of Sennacherib (Chicago, 1924).

Wisdom Literature

O. R. Gurney, "The Tale of the Poor Man of Nippur" in Anatolian Studies 6 (1956), 145-64.

W. G. Lambert, "The Poem of the Righteous Sufferer Ludlul Bēl Nēmeqi" in Babylonian Wisdom Literature, 21-62; "The Babylonian Theodicy" in ibid., 63-91; "The Dialogue of Pessimism" in ibid., 139-49.

Articles of Interest

Articles of interest concerning Akkadian and Mesopotamia in general may be found in scholarly journals such as JANES (Journal of the Ancient Near Eastern Society of Columbia University), JAOS (Journal of the American Oriental Society), JCS (Journal of Cuneiform Studies), JNES (Journal of Near Eastern Studies), Orientalia, RA (Revue d'assyriologie), and ZA (Zeitschrift für Assyriologie). These articles, together with books and monographs of interest, have now been conveniently indexed by R. Borger in his indispensible Handbuch der Keilschriftliteratur (Berlin, 1967 & 1975).

General Works

M. A. Beek, Atlas of Mesopotamia (N.Y. & London, 1962).

The Cambridge Ancient History, revised edition of volumes 1 & 2 (Cambridge, 1970-).

E. Chiera, They Wrote on Clay, Phoenix edition (Chicago, 1956).

H. Frankfort, The Art and Architecture of the Ancient Orient (Harmondsworth, 1954).

H. Frankfort, Th. Jacobsen, et al., Before Philosophy, Penguin edition (Harmondsworth, 1951).

W. W. Hallo & W. K. Simpson, The Ancient Near East (N.Y., 1971).

A. Heidel, The Babylonian Genesis, Phoenix edition (Chicago, 1963).

A. Heidel, The Gilgamesh Epic and Old Testament Parallels, Phoenix edition (Chicago, 1963).

T. Jones, The Sumerian Problem (N.Y., 1969).

S. N. Kramer, History Begins at Sumer, Anchor edition (N.Y., 1959).

S. N. Kramer, The Sumerians (Chicago, 1963).

A. L. Oppenheim, Ancient Mesopotamia, Phoenix edition (Chicago, 1964).

A. L. Oppenheim, Letters From Mesopotamia (Chicago, 1967).

S. A. Pallis, The Antiquity of Iraq (Copenhagen, 1956).

J. B. Pritchard, ed., Ancient Near Eastern Texts Relating to the Old Testament, 3rd edition (Princeton, 1969).

G. Roux, Ancient Iraq, Pelican edition (Harmondsworth, 1966).

H. W. F. Saggs, The Greatness That Was Babylon (N.Y., 1962).

E. Strommenger, 5000 Years of the Art of Mesopotamia (N.Y., n.d.).